true stories by **Siegfried Kra**, M.D.

DANCER *in the* Garden

PLEASURE BOAT STUDIO: A LITERARY PRESS

ISBN 978-0-912887-61-6

Library of Congress Control Number:
2019934538

Design by Lauren Grosskopf

*Pleasure Boat Studio books are available
through your favorite bookstore and through the following*:
SPD (Small Press Distribution) 800-869-7553
Baker & Taylor 800-775-1100
Ingram 615-793-5000
amazon.com and bn.com
& PLEASURE BOAT STUDIO: A LITERARY PRESS
www.pleasureboatstudio.com
Pleasboatpublishing@gmail.com
Seattle, Washington

These stories are based on Dr. Kra's actual case studies and other events. Certain names have been changed.

OTHER WORKS *by*
DR. SIEGFRIED KRA

Twilight in Danzig

Second Edition, A Novel / Historical Fiction

Pleasure Boat Studio, 2018

❖

Twilight in Danzig: A Privileged Jewish
Childhood During the Third Reich

First Edition, Nonfiction / Autobiography

Canal House, 2015

❖

The Collected Stories from a Doctor's Notebook

1st Edition; CreateSpace Independent Publishing, 2014

❖

How to Keep Your Husband Alive: An Empowerment Tool
for Women Who Care About Their Man's Health

Lebhar-Friedman, 2001

❖

Physical Diagnosis: A Concise Textbook

Elsevier Science Ltd, 1987

❖

What Every Woman Must Know About Heart Disease:
A No-nonsense Approach to Diagnosing, Treating,
and Preventing the #1 Killer of Women

Grand Central Publishing, 1997

Coronary Bypass Surgery: Who Needs It

W W Norton & Co Inc, 1987

❖

Aging Myths: Reversible Causes of Mind and Memory Loss

McGraw-Hill, 1986

❖

The Good Heart Diet Cook Book

Ellen Stern, Jonathan Michaels & Siegfried J. Kra

Ticknor and Fields, 1982

❖

Examine Your Doctor:

A patient's guide to avoiding medical mishaps

Houghton Mifflin Co International Inc., 1984

❖

Is Surgery Necessary?

Macmillan, 1981

❖

The Three-Legged Stallion: And Other Tales

W. W. Norton and Company, Inc., 1980

❖

Basic Correlative Echocardiography

Technique and Interpretation

Medical Examination Publishing Company; 2nd edition, 1977

DANCER
in the
Garden

For my daughters, LISETTE & ANNICE

CONTENTS

❖ *Preface* ❖

I RECENTLY REACHED THE MILESTONE OF FIFTY YEARS OF practicing medicine, and I am astounded to realize that I've been a cardiologist for that long. Over the decades, I have had more than my share of truly extraordinary medical experiences—not only among the 200,000 patients who have come under my care during that time, but for myself as well. I have published some of these accounts in newspapers and magazines and in two previous collections. But more and more of these tales began to crowd my thoughts and insist on being told. Some were so painful I simply couldn't bear to write them until now.

I feel lucky and grateful to still be practicing medicine as I pass eighty years of age, and to continue to treat some patients who have been coming to me for decades. I am an avid tennis player, and still manage to fit in a match or two nearly every day. In addition to my thriving clinical practice, I am an Associate Professor at the Yale School of Medicine, and for ten years I had a weekly radio segment on NPR called "Heart to Heart Talk."

But it has not been an easy road for me. My father was a wealthy coal dealer in Danzig, Germany, when the Nazis came to power. Most of our extended family would perish at their hands, but we escaped from Gestapo headquarters (my father, my mother, my older brother, and I), and fled to America in 1938, when I was a child of eight. We left a fifteen-room house in Germany with maids and chauffeurs for a hand-to-mouth existence in a New York tenement.

My father was reduced to shoveling snow or separating zippers from old clothing (at ten cents per rescued zipper) to make a meager living. I took odd jobs: delivery boy, housecleaner, usher (I once escorted Henry Fonda to his seat and he tipped me a quarter). I taught myself English and worked my way through college, eventually attending medical school in France and Switzerland and then at Yale.

We were among the lucky Jews who escaped. Many would become great scientists, composers, doctors, film directors, judges—in essence bringing thousands of years of culture to America. It was the reason I heard Polish and German spoken frequently in the New York City streets of my youth.

I know what it means to be poor, to go to bed hungry, to be deeply lonely, and to have a close brush with death. Among other dangers, I have survived scarlet fever, a pulmonary embolism, a near-sinking aboard a merchant ship, a plane crash, and waking up to my house burning around me. All this in addition to the usual lost loves, broken hearts, and sometimes shocking realities of life as an M.D.

I have been privileged to know thousands upon thousands of patients, some more colorful than others whose stories I include in these pages. There were the ones who had been given cocaine as treatment by a previous doctor, the ones who threatened my life, the one who had a heart attack while driving me to the airport, and a few of dubious occupation who helped sustain me in my early years. Perhaps most shocking was the nun who made an astonishing choice. I am grateful to all of them for making me a better doctor, and I am pleased to share their stories with you here.

These vignettes span the years from 1939 to 2011, and all are true stories that happened to me or to a patient I knew. I can't help but remark in some of them on the passing of the golden age of medicine, when doctors were more revered than today and when treating patients meant spending time with them and listening to what they needed to say. They are not all, strictly speaking, tales of love, but they are incidents that affected me deeply—and I hope they will affect you deeply, too.

I have had a delightful romantic life, but from time to time over the years I would ask myself whether I have truly loved and been loved. I met my first love in New York when I was a teenager. In college I was in love with a pony-tailed ballet student for four whole weeks. I loved a patient of mine when I was in medical school and a mysterious woman who lived in the Toulouse rooming house where I learned to study medical texts in French. My wife left me in middle age, and a new woman entered my life for a time. A younger girlfriend later suffered a debiLana'sting chronic disease. Did any of these women truly love me? I don't suppose I will ever have a satisfactory answer, but I have learned not to ask for proof but to be content with the love I have felt, past and present.

And I am not the only one. A few years ago I received a phone call from a woman in Australia who wanted to tell me she still had the book of Keats poetry I had inscribed for her sixty years earlier, when I was fifteen.

One of the responsibilities of practicing cardiology is that you are continually making life and death decisions. It leaves no time or inclination for self-pity or regret. When I do feel nostalgic, I'm usually sorry I hadn't kept in closer touch with my friends, many of whom are gone now. I have two wonderful daughters and a treasure trove of memories from half a century in medicine, which I am adding to every day. I still write, still teach, still play a mean game of tennis, and still marvel at the pleasures and dangers that one life can bring.

I take care of people's hearts so they can go on loving. I can think of no greater privilege.

HOLDING MY BROTHER'S HAND

2011

Gloved, masked, dressed in a plastic dress with a funny-looking plastic hat as if going to a Halloween party, he instead finds himself in a bright room without any decoration. A jumble of sounds reaches his failing ears: steadily dripping fluids from bags hanging at his side, the hissing, whistling, and blowing of unfamiliar machines, indistinct voices. Young people masked and gowned peer at blinking computers, ignoring him.

He is lying on a bed, strapped down like a prisoner with leather straps. There are tubes in his mouth, tubes in his neck, tubes in his stomach. They stand over him, so many in this cold cubicle with no windows, speaking as if he were not there. One of the gowned women raises the bed sheets and looks at his flaccid penis, also connected to a tube. She checks the boots, large as a cowboy's, riding up his legs to prevent clots from forming. Around the necks of the other young masked and gowned people hang long black tubes called stethoscopes, once used to listen to the heart, now mere decoration. For with all the monitoring equipment, there is no space on his chest to place a stethoscope. Even if there were, it would be hard to hear his beating heart above the beeping of the machines.

Another machine is wheeled into the room and all the young masked and gowned people step out and, zip, an X-ray is taken. Then another machine scans the chest, and he can see flashing pictures on the screen.

He groans and moves around, fighting to loosen his strapped hands.

Someone says, "Don't do that."

"Is he deaf?" another says.

Still no one approaches him, as if he has a contagious disease.

"Does he understand English?"

"He's probably demented."

I walk into the cubicle just as the word "demented" is uttered, another gowned and masked person, but no longer young.

The man lying on the table is three days post-op after a complex operation: two fistulas, or holes, repaired. Although semi-conscious, he moves his head as he is going to be extubated.

One of the masked and gowned people says "he looks good" in a tone of authority, standing by the door.

Still no one touches him as the tube is pulled up out of his throat. He coughs.

Another yells, "How do you feel?"

He does not answer but again begins to fight his restraints, pulling at them, making sounds like a trapped animal. He is partially deaf. He is not demented. He is a practicing attorney. He is my brother.

I take my gloves off, take his hand in mine and squeeze it. He responds with a nod of his head and becomes calm and subdued.

His wife failed to mention that he was deaf. After the operation, she and her son were afraid to hold his hand or his head.

"Just touch him," I tell the masked and gloved figures. "Hold his hand and it will give him a feeling of comfort and security. He won't be so frightened. It's an old method I learned in medical school, before you had all these machines." All medical care should include the ancient bedside practice of taking the patient's hand. "It works better than Xanax," I tell them.

I squeeze my brother's hand and do not let go.

PLANE CRASH
on a FROZEN LAKE
1982

THE MORNING OF FEBRUARY 21, 1982, WAS GRAY AND dreary. I was making arrangements for a trip to Boston and upstate New York as part of a lecture publicity tour for my recently published book. All morning I felt uneasy, restless, and exhausted. I was peculiarly reluctant to leave. Perhaps it was the comfort of Sunday morning, surrounded by my chatty, cheerful family at the breakfast table.

I had been booked to leave from the New Haven airport at six that evening, but I had an 8:00 a.m. TV show to do. I decided to leave earlier and arrive in Boston in time to settle in before bedtime. I thought of canceling. I told my wife that I was worn out.

"I am coming down with a virus," I said. "My stomach feels upset."

"You really love to go on these tours," she said reassuringly. "You'll see, once you get on that plane and to Boston, you'll be yourself again. And in the morning, in front of the cameras, you'll be on a high—you're a born ham."

She was right, of course. I always found it exhilarating

to be front and center. Even though these tours harvest few book sales, I really enjoy the notoriety. And while they only last a few days at a time, they offer a change from my tumultuous medical practice.

The day was unusually warm for the end of February. A slight drizzle started as I arrived at the airport. Waiting to board, I saw a little girl in a blue coat embrace her mother and then run out to the plane. I wondered why anyone would allow such a small child to travel by herself. I embraced my wife and daughter and felt a bit sad, and terribly uneasy. I suddenly wished I had driven to Boston, but then I'd have had to drive to Syracuse and Rochester and Buffalo.

An experienced traveler, I always request the seat behind the pilot on these small Otter planes. It makes me feel more secure. Snaking myself down the narrow aisle, I caught a glimpse of some of my fellow passengers. There was a tall black man. A mother and her son were in the seat opposite mine. The little girl in the blue coat sat next to a young man at the back of the plane. There were twelve passengers on this fully booked flight. My raincoat was on my lap, as was my briefcase, which contained a new manuscript I was working on.

Once we were airborne, I spread the manuscript on my lap. From the window I could see New Haven Harbor, covered by an eerie-looking mist. There were two pilots. One was giving the usual in-flight instructions to the passengers, which were terribly garbled because of a defective PA system.

I wondered why pilots were always so tall and strong-looking, and charming. They gave me confidence and trust, making these small commuter planes seem somehow more substantial.

"Well, folks, we should arrive in Boston in forty-five minutes," the senior pilot informed us cheerfully just as the windshield began being pelted with rain. I placed the manuscript pages back into their folder, returned it to my briefcase, and sat back, trying to relax.

I tried to plan what I was going to say on this next interview. But instead I began to wonder if I would die in a plane crash. I had been fortunate so far, having traveled hundreds of times without mishap. But what if the odds were turning against me?

My own death had not really preoccupied me until then, although as a cardiologist death is my constant companion. How many times had I stood by a bedside and witnessed the last moments of a human life? Everyone dies the same way, unlike births, which are all different. The last gasp of life is a universal phenomenon, regardless of the cause. Death is the end of a personality. Being a custodian of human lives, I am programmed to save them. This is as much a part of my brain as eating and sleeping. But who would try to save mine when the time came? Who saves the doctors?

I took a comb from my jacket pocket and began to straighten my hair, arrange my tie, smooth the blazer I was wearing, as if I were grooming for a party.

My eyes were transfixed by the windshield. The wipers were moving, large, thin blades that looked like long spider legs gliding back and forth, back and forth, across the glass. How could the pilots see through all the fog and mist? Then I realized that they were flying by the instruments before them.

Suddenly the wipers stopped moving in the middle of

the windshield, like a movie that abruptly freezes a frame of the action. In seconds, ice formed on the glass, and I saw the pilots' strained looks as they started pulling and pushing different levers. I stretched out my arms in front of me. Did anyone else sense that terror was about to strike? The woman behind me who was about my age? The little girl? The secretive German traveler, who held onto his briefcase as if all his valuables were inside?

First came a faint odor, almost imperceptible, but somehow familiar to me. It was not disagreeable. It began to grow until I recognized an unmistakable smell I meet each day in my office, in the hospital, in the operating room: alcohol. Behind me, the passengers remained oblivious, comfortable, safe.

A little puff of smoke started to curl around the cockpit, slowly increasing, and in minutes the entire cockpit was hidden behind a thick blue miasma. The smoke made my breathing more and more labored, as if I were submerged under water. The passengers began to stir. Sleepy eyes now stared in disbelief and fear. Voices grew louder, "What the hell is going on? Seconds later, little bursts of flame appeared from the instrument panel, fire being spit by a dragon. The fire spread, licking the walls, the cockpit. I threw my raincoat at the fire. It was ablaze in seconds. The smoke increased. I began to gasp for air. I sat back and waited. We would not survive much longer without fresh air.

Is this what my family felt in their final moments in the concentration camp in Treblinka? The Germans didn't get me, but the gods would finally have their way. I wouldn't get to see my children married or make the bestseller list. The cabin had grown hot, dark, suffocating.

"How long can you withstand low-oxygen concentration in the blood," the professor asked me on the final exam, "before brain damage occurs?"

Someone shouted, "Where is the fire extinguisher?" and grabbed my tennis racket. This was a pressurized plane. We can't break a window, I thought. We mustn't. But someone did, smashing at the glass until it gave. The pilots were festooned in flames, but one of the ghastly figures stuck his head out the smashed window as the plane dove at a steep angle, shuddering and rattling. Death was upon us. I could see mountains, ice-covered mountains.

I'm in Switzerland again, in the very attic where I lived as a medical school student. There is no heat or hot water in my room, just a little electric stove, and it is a frigid winter. There is a small bed and desk, my open books upon it. Next door lives Klaus, also a student. On his desk are pictures of his father standing next to Hitler.

"Were you in the war, Klaus?" I ask.

"Yes," he answers me in German. "I was in the submarine service. I knew nothing of what went on. My father was Hitler's friend, a close friend."

Klaus and I often share coffee and exchange notes. One morning he is found dead, having jumped from the bridge in the center of town.

Suddenly the mountains are covered with a blinding bright yellow light. I squint to see. I hear soft voices. It is so peaceful, the most peaceful moment of my entire life, absolute serenity. I am floating above the plane, an objective observer calmly watching it burn.

I must have passed out—or had I died? The plane was on the ground. I unfastened my seatbelt, moved my arms and legs. There was no pain anywhere, only heat and stifling smoke. I lurched out of my seat. There was moaning and screaming around me, the sounds of disaster, as I tried to run to the back of the plane. The exit door was blocked. I cleared it, then kicked it until it flew open. A tall man standing behind me dove out of the open door like a swimmer diving into a pool. Lying at my feet was the little girl with the blue coat, shrieking. Her face was covered with blood. I grabbed her by her coat and dragged her out with me as I struggled to leave the burning plane. I touched ground. It was hard and icy cold. It must have snowed, I thought. I dragged the girl along the ice, away from the blazing plane.

"Stop pulling me," she screamed, "you are hurting my back!"

"Everything is okay, you're fine," I said, the doctor speaking. The man was terrified.

Suddenly one of the pilots appeared, black as charcoal, weaving from side to side as if drunk. His leg was ripped and bleeding.

"Get away from the plane!" I heard someone shout. Passengers were crawling, staggering away. The little girl in the blue coat stood and walked. A young woman, arms outstretched before her, was feeling her way.

"I can't see!" she screamed. I took her arm and escorted her away from the inferno. Her face was wet and red, her eyes swollen shut. We moved slowly, a grotesque march from hell. Now a terrible explosion, as if planets had collided. Then an ugly pile of acrid-smelling, burning debris was all that was left of Pilgrim Flight 458 headed for Boston. That same sense of utter peace I had experienced when the conflagration began returned. Still I felt no pain, though I knew I'd been injured. There was no numbness. My knee was swollen to the touch, and my ankle looked black. We could all feel the warmth from the burning plane. Was I still alive? The young woman placed her arm in mine.

"I'm so scared. Please! I don't see anything. Where are we?"

"You are fine," I reassured her. "We are saved. Don't worry. I'm a doctor. I will take care of you."

"Are you really a doctor? Oh, thank God! God sent you to me."

What I thought at first was frozen ground was a lake, a frozen lake on a warm day. Somehow we had to cross this icy surface to safety. I strained my eyes to spot the shore and thought I saw it a long way off. If the ice were to give, the blind girl clutching my arm with all her strength would pull me down, and I too would drown. I could have left her to wander off by herself, to save my own life. I was well enough to make it to shore. But I had never abandoned a sick person in my life, and surely wouldn't now.

"We have to walk very carefully," I told her softly. "We're on a frozen lake, but the ice seems spongy, wet. Walk carefully, step carefully."

Her grip on me grew tighter. She took small steps, brought her feet down daintily, as if she were walking on eggs.

"Just pretend that we are walking in the park on a nice fall day and that everything is safe and beautiful," I said softly. "We are lucky to have survived the plane crash. You will tell your grandchildren of that one day."

Our stroll continued, like two lovers arm in arm. Each

step could mean the end of us both. I felt the patches of soft ice move slightly below our feet, but the lake remained frozen despite the warm air. The plane, we were later told, had crashed right in the center of the frozen lake. I never felt the impact. The plane slid and sailed a thousand feet across the ice before the nose gently dipped into the lake, a huge bird taking a drink. One of the wings of the plane had broken off. We approached it on our promenade across the lake. The bird's wing lay flat on the ice, smoldering. I watched it slowly begin to sink and disappear below the surface. I didn't tell my blind escort what was happening, but she heard the terrifying hiss it made and the swishing sound as the reluctant wing was drawn to its icy grave.

"What was that?" she asked in panic.

"It's the wind, nothing more. We'll be on the shore soon. We'll be safe." Now I could clearly see the shore. On the banks of this lake of death were some young boys, standing, watching, but no one else to help.

"Walk towards the other edge!" they yelled. "It is all melted here."

We changed our course like mariners sailing the dark sea. Now I saw that others had already reached land. They urged us on. We approached shore, and the ice became soft as pudding. It reminded me of how I once crossed the streets in New York as a child. First stepping on the ice on the edge of the sidewalk and then suddenly being in water, slush. Three young boys came to the very edge of the lake with their arms outstretched. We were entering water now. The young woman clutched me ever more tightly as, with each step, we began to sink. The icy water reached my thigh. It felt like hot moss. One more step. Safety was five feet away. I threw her with all my strength, and the three boys grabbed her by the arm, pulled her out. I struggled to get to land, the water almost reaching my shoulder. Another step. Another. The boys had me. A mighty pull.

Soaking wet, I began to feel terribly cold. We walked, the three boys leading us through thick vines. Surely this must be a beautiful spot in the spring: yellow forsythia in full bloom, framing the lake. We then climbed over a barbed-wire fence, and now we were on the road. I looked back. We had cheated the Lady of the Lake.

One of the pilots was lying on the ground, a terrible pile of charcoal, unconscious.

"He is the doctor!" someone yelled.

I struggled over to the pilot's body. He was still alive. What did they expect me to do? Here? Now? It took twenty dreadful minutes for an ambulance to arrive. Isolated from the world, we had crashed in the Scituate Reservoir in Rhode Island, a body of water that had rarely ever frozen, no less on a day when the temperature was 50 degrees.

They packed me in the ambulance with the burned pilot, the blind young woman, and a mother and son, who both suffered bone fractures and head injuries. In his haste, one of the ambulance attendants forgot to close the back door, and as we sped off we began to slip toward the gaping hole, like children in a park on a slide. I held fast to the stretcher nestling the unconscious but groaning man. The others were screaming for the ambulance to stop, but the driver did not hear our plea. In desperation I grabbed a bottle of saline solution from a rack and threw it at the window separating us from the driver. He turned his head toward us and was horrified to see us hanging on for our very lives. He stopped and closed the door securely.

For the rest of the trip, as the ambulance raced toward Rhode Island Hospital, I felt helpless trying to give some comfort to this poor man who was burned over at least 75 percent of his body. He had been a great hero; so had his co-pilot. He had brought the plane down while his body was encased in flames, somehow steering it with his head outside the window. None of us on that flight will ever forget him. Both pilots would receive awards for their heroic acts. Those of us who survived (two would not) realized that a miracle had occurred.

After the longest ride of my life, we finally arrived at the emergency room. I walked out of the ambulance against the warning shouts of the emergency-room staff to wait for help.

"Don't bother with me," I said, "I'm fine." I walked toward the cafeteria while other patients looked on as if I were mad.

"Doctor, you must sign in and be examined. You just survived a plane crash!" the nurse shouted at me.

I gave her a derisive smile, and said, "All I want is a hamburger. I haven't had one in years, since I've been on a damned low-cholesterol diet."

I was hungry. Famished. I felt as if I hadn't eaten in weeks. The adrenaline was overflowing. I ate three hamburgers and then called my wife.

"Don't get worried, you probably heard of the crash. If you didn't, turn on the radio. Come and get me. Bring a coat, a hat, and a bottle of scotch."

When my wife and daughter arrived, I was lying on a stretcher being examined by an intern. They did not know what to expect, and both burst into tears of joy when they saw that I was in one piece. Much to the dismay of the emergency-room staff, I grabbed the scotch and drank to my heart's content. My knee was injured, but I refused to stay in the hospital. As I was leaving the emergency room, Jeremy Geidt, a Shakespearean actor from the Yale Repertory Theater, approached me to thank me for pulling his daughter off the plane. She was the little girl in the blue coat.

The press swarmed, vultures lusting to hear from me about the crash, especially because I was a doctor. I did get my day on TV, and the coverage was better than my publishers ever dreamed. Coast to coast, on every network, in the morning, at night, I was interviewed and quoted.

I took a long overdue vacation from my practice. My knee was badly injured, and I limped around in an Ace bandage. I consulted a physician who prescribed painkillers, which I threw away. I had one physical therapy session. What I needed most, and did not receive from the medical profession, was a kind word of understanding. Instead, one doctor said, "You will be disabled for several months, and don't be disappointed if you can't play tennis again. Swimming is much better for you anyhow. You're getting too old to play tennis. You should know all this, being a cardiologist."

Tennis had been one of my grand pleasures in life, which only another athlete could really understand. The tennis racket had even saved our lives when one of the passengers used it to break the windows of the plane. He was a flight engineer. Who else would have thought of breaking windows in flight?

Doctors feel uncomfortable treating other doctors, and I resented their cold approach. I consulted a neurologist to be certain I had no neurological damage to my brain. But doctors feel uncomfortable being treated by other doctors, too: I was embarrassed to tell him that during the height of the crash I had seen that bright light that many people describe seeing in a near-death experience. One of my colleagues checked out my cardiovascular system and declared it normal. Yet I did not feel normal. I felt separated from the world, a visitor, an observer.

Once my father had given me boxing lessons, and then I had been matched up against another boy. I had been beaten up miserably and had staggered out of the ring, dazed. That is how I felt for weeks after the crash. Yet I felt docile, peaceful.

"How is it possible," the federal investigator asked me, "that you did not get one burn on your body when you were sitting immediately behind the flaming cockpit? The woman who sat behind you was burned to death. It took days to identify her body. These were among many unanswerable questions that unnerved me. Why had the reservoir been frozen? It had not frozen over for as long as the natives in the area could recall. And why did I have such a strong premonition of danger that day? I am not given to superstitious feelings.

Two passengers on that plane died. I am a scientist and had difficulty accepting that any master plan for my survival existed in heaven. The rabbi of my synagogue said that I had been tested. God had too many other agendas to be concentrating on me, I told the rabbi.

But for his great and sincere concern, I contributed to the synagogue—and to the church, too. Just in case.

GABRIELLE'S DANCE

1952

THE TRAIN RIDE FROM LAUSANNE TO LEYSIN TOOK forty-five minutes, winding through the beautiful valleys of the Swiss Alps. It was the winter of 1952, and I was heading to a famous tuberculosis sanatorium located atop a magnificent Alpine mountain. The air there was clear and dry, and the mountain was covered by miles of sparkling white snow. Everything, including the sanatorium, was gleaming white, except for the elevator—a black freight elevator that carried visitors up and the dead back down the mountain to the train that would take them to Lausanne.

I was one of fifteen medical students crowded into this vertical moving bus, which held a sharp medicinal smell. We had come to learn about TB, a much feared and terribly contagious disease that had already killed millions. We felt anxious and afraid, noticing little of the beauty around us.

A nurse met us as we stepped off the elevator and escorted us to the lecture hall. It looked like the rotunda I'd seen in other medical schools, except this one was enclosed in glass through which we could see a white paradise of glistening snow and the majestic surrounding mountains. The lecturer who was going to give us a preliminary talk on TB looked like a giraffe in a long white coat.

"I'm Professor Durand," he announced. "I have TB, mostly cured, and I have been in this sanatorium since I was a medical student, like you."

Every year, at least one student contracted TB and was forced into a sanatorium. In this age before antibiotics had been discovered, the only common treatment consisted of the "open-air method": rest and exposure to the sun. Alternatives included drastic surgical treatment, such as pumping air into the stomach or chest to collapse the diseased lung, or attempts to cut the TB cavity free from the lung.

Outside on a large open terrace, patients in underclothes were strewn on long folding chairs, lying in the sun like skiers resting between slaloms.

I was assigned two patients. Madame Fabron was in her sixties, and Gabrielle was twenty-three. Each patient had a private room off a long white corridor, and each door had a plaque bearing the name of its tenant.

I knocked on Madame Coron's door and a pleasant voice told me to come in. Sitting by the window was a gray-haired woman, knitting, wearing a colorful shawl around her narrow shoulders. "*Entrez*. Please come in and close the door. We don't want a draft, do we?" she said.

"I am the new medical student assigned to examine you."

"Oh, I know, it is the beginning of the month."

"You speak English very well," I told her.

"Thank you. I taught myself. I have the time to do it. Please sit down. Would you like a glass of champagne? It is nearly lunch."

"Thank you, but it is too early for me."

"Ah, yes, you Americans live by the clock. There is a time to eat, to drink, to sleep, to work, and perhaps there is a time to die, but you are too young to understand all that."

As she poured a glass of champagne for herself, my eyes roamed around the richly furnished room. Ottoman bro-caded fabrics and silks upholstered the chairs and benches, and colorful spreads covered the floor. On the walls hung calligraphies of embroidered silk designs displayed in vivid colors. I felt I was in the room of a sixteenth-century sultan.

"My family are Turks, Ottomans," she said, noticing my reaction. "I was born in Istanbul."

Outside the room was a large balcony with a blue velvet chaise longue covered by a large canvas to protect it from the rain.

"We have to sit outside on the balcony three hours a day, and when the weather permits, the doctor asks us to sleep outside several times a week. But I am getting too old for such acrobatics.

"Now, my young American student, take a chair here and I will answer your questions."

With pad and pencil in hand, I started the routine of taking a medical history.

"How old are you?"

"The last time I counted I was sixty-one. If it weren't for you students, I would have lost count long ago."

"When was the first time you became ill?"

"Thirty-five years ago, before you were born."

"You have had TB for thirty-five years?"

"Perhaps longer. I was married and lived in the Topkapi Palace in Istanbul. When my child was six years old, I became ill."

"How long have you been in Leysin?"

"Twenty-five years. The doctors said I was not to leave if I wanted to stay alive." She continued to talk without my needing to ask her questions, and after one hour I had scribbled ten pages of notes.

"I am getting tired," she finally said. "Let us continue tomorrow. It is time for lunch."

The students ate their meals in the same cafeteria used for the staff and visitors. I joined the other students, and we shared stories of our first encounters with TB patients. I was reluctant to eat the food at first because we all knew the TB bacilli pervaded everything, but the others didn't seem to share my fears and so I tried to relax and eat.

After lunch I visited the next patient. Her room was located in Ward B, on the other side of the hospital. This, I was told, was where the very sick patients were placed, some of whom were just waiting to die. It was at the end of a long hall that smelled of disinfectant.

One of the students informed me that the disinfectant had seeped into the hall from one of the rooms where a patient had died. It had to be cleaned and made ready for the next tenant. A stretcher passed by, with a white sheet covering a body. Deceased patients were carried down to the basement, where an autopsy would be performed. Then they were placed in a sealed brown box and taken down the mountain in the freight elevator to a special compartment on the train and back home to be buried. The coffins remained sealed because TB remained alive in the dead patients.

In this ward the patients had numbers, not names, on their doors. When I knocked on Gabrielle's door there was no response, so I meekly opened it. Inside a young woman lay on a bed under a white sheet. Her eyes were closed, and she had long beautiful brown hair spread out on a large pillow like a fan. As I was about to leave she spoke in a sweet voice in French, saying, "Don't go away. I was only resting. I become so tired after lunch. I was outside all day on the deck. I hate being inside when the sun is out. Are you one of the doctors?"

My French was good, but I carried a very strong accent. "I am one of the students," I said, "here to examine you."

The room was stark and depressing. There was nothing except a bed, a night table, and a commode with an empty urinal on the floor. A clipboard hung from the wall, keeping a daily record of the patient's temperature. With my other patient, I had felt intimidated by the luxurious surroundings and her familiarity with my task. But this poor young soul was afraid, shy, and vulnerable. She lay in the bed like a wounded bird, and she appeared so desperately pale I was afraid she was going to die in front of me, something I could not bear to witness. Doctors have to steel themselves against such possibilities, but as a medical student I knew I would be devastated by the patients who didn't make it.

Gently, ever so softly, I moved the bare chair next to her bed and stood next to it. "I am an American medical student. My French is good but not perfect, so be patient with me, and don't speak too fast, because then I won't understand you and you will have to repeat everything."

She laughed. "I can understand you. Don't be afraid of me. You can sit down. I won't make you sick, but if I become tired you will have to come back tomorrow."

Finally, I sat on the chair, sniffing the air, which smelled of the disinfectant rising from the floor.

"They just scoured the floor with that disgusting fluid," Gabrielle said. "It is good to rest. Every day I look to be stronger; instead I feel worse. Is that what is supposed to happen?"

"It takes time to get better. You must be patient," I told her in an unconvincing voice.

"How old are you?" I started on the traditional routine of history taking.

"Twenty-three." Her eyes were like two light gemstones, soft, transparent like the faint lines of a Degas painting.

"How long have you been ill?"

"I am not sure. It was so long ago." Her cheeks were pale except for two jolly red circles. She kept tugging at the sheet to bring it up to her narrow neck, as if to hide herself from me.

"I became ill on Easter day with a bad cold and it didn't improve. My father took me to the doctor and they X-rayed my chest, and here I am. Simple as that. So it must be six months. Time stands still on the mountains; only the light changes." As she spoke her voice was interrupted by a violent cough and then she began to wheeze.

"Are you all right?" I asked.

"I start to cough when I speak for too long. I used to love to talk, sometimes too much. When I lived at home with my parents and two younger sisters, they complained that I never stopped chatting. 'You are a chatterbox,' my mother would tell me."

"Are you a student?" I asked.

"Yes. I dance."

Her face turned a shade of red that reminded me of begonias in bloom. "It must be early afternoon," she said, "because that is when my fever comes to visit me and stays all night until the first light of day. My body then feels as it did when I would dance, warm and sweaty, and my heart pounds. I used to be so afraid when it happened, but now it makes me sleepy. I fall into a deep, peaceful sleep and dream. Oh, do I dream! I dream I am dancing on top of the mountain in the cool air, and everything smells good, instead of like disinfectant."

The nurse came into the room carrying a tray with a thermometer and lubricant. "Well, I am glad to see you getting on so well with Gabrielle," she said. "Turn over, my little ballerina, time for your afternoon forecast. Doctor, you can step outside and have a smoke or something."

"Will you come back?" Gabrielle asked.

"Of course, but I will have to make the five o'clock train."

From outside the door I could hear Gabrielle's gentle voice. "Can't you warm it up? Why do you have to stick it in there? You know it will be high. Put it under my armpit. It is just as accurate."

"Gabrielle, the doctor wants a rectal temperature."

Five minutes later the nurse let me back in and gave me a sad, knowing look as she pointed to the clipboard.

"What was it?" Gabrielle asked. "No, wait, let me guess…104. Right? I can tell because I am becoming drowsy."

"Here, take two aspirins with a little water and you will cool down," the nurse said. "When you are ready to examine her, Doctor, push this bell, and I will assist you."

"Thank you, but I still have to finish the history," I explained.

"Oh, good," Gabrielle said cheerfully, "then you will have to return tomorrow and I will be all fresh and cleaned." The nurse placed a small glass filled with a purple solution on her night table.

"It is theophylline," the nurse said to me. "You take it, Gabrielle, and don't spill it out into the sink. You know it helps your wheezing. Doctor, see to it she drinks it. It opens her bronchial tubes."

"I hate it," the patient complained. "What good is it? It only works for a few hours and then I wheeze again."

"Gabrielle, would you prefer a suppository?"

"I will drink the purple poison, thank you."

She folded her slender milk-white arms in front of her after the nurse left and said, "Well, go ahead, ask me questions."

Before, her eyes had looked cool and youthful; now they were partially closed and wet. Her body was burning up from the fever. She had small narrow eyebrows that curved gently above her drooping eyelids, as if someone had sketched them in.

"Where were you born?"

"In the Valais, in Sion. Have you ever been there?"

"No."

"Then you must visit it before you return to New York."

"How do you know I am from New York?"

"I guessed. I know of only three cities in America: New York, Chicago, and Hollywood."

"Well, you are right, I am from New York. Did you have any childhood diseases?"' I continued.

"Yes: scarletina, mumps, chicken pox, and something else that made my cough sound like a horn, not like the kind I have now."

"Whooping cough?"

"That's it."

I glanced at my watch. It was nearing five. "I have to go, Gabrielle, or I will miss my train."

"Come tomorrow after breakfast. My room number is 26, so don't get lost. There are many Gabrielles at Leysin."

"I will remember the number. Have a good night's rest."

"Can you open the window a little before you leave so I can hear your train depart? I love to hear the train; it gives me hope that someday I will be on it. Here in Leysin we live by sound and light and smell, because the mountains are always the same. Only these things are different. The mountains are my jailkeepers, but the sounds of the train are the sounds of hope."

As I closed her door I felt an intensely sad pang in my chest. The train back to Lausanne was crowded with medical students, nurses, and doctors who were free for the evening. As eager as they were to leave for the city, so I yearned to stay with Gabrielle to look after her. What if she wheezed and coughed bitterly at night, and there was no one to hear? Being isolated like a punished child in a miserable dreary room was bad medical care. She only had a bell to ring for help, but that was hundreds of yards away from the nurses' station.

Next to me on the train sat a student from Zurich who was in his senior year, as I was. His specialty was going to be TB and respiratory diseases. "How do you like our Leysin?" he asked in English.

"I find it fascinating and sad."

"We give them excellent care, and most of our patients recover. Dr. Jacquet's treatment has been successful for ninety percent of our inpatients. Our sanatorium has the best record of any in Europe. It is even better than your famous one in Saratoga. What part of the sanatorium are you visiting?"

I told him about Madame Fabron and Gabrielle.

"Gabrielle is one of our most serious cases."

"Will she die?"

"She has not responded to Jacquet's treatment as well as we had hoped. At least, not yet."

I spent the remainder of the evening in the quiet of my room reading everything I could find on TB. The signs of worsening TB are persistent fever, continual weight loss, gross spitting up of blood, and the TB lung cavity not shrinking. As I read, the image of Gabrielle's innocent red-cheeked face seemed to fill the page and I could hear her wheezing. That night I had a fretful sleep.

At seven o'clock the next morning I was back on the train to Leysin. I was the only medical student on board, along with the nurses and doctors and other helpers. It was the end of November and the mountain air was damp. The clouds hung over the mountains like white curtains.

Ward B was deserted except for two orderlies pushing a stretcher with a body under a white sheet. I stopped short and wanted to pull the sheet back. Instead I rushed to Room 26 and found the door ajar. I slowly nudged it open and, with great joy and relief, saw Gabrielle sitting up in bed reading a book of poems by Verlaine.

"*Bonjour*," I rejoiced.

"Aren't you a little early?" she said.

"I like to get an early start."

Her face was pale, and her eyes looked like transparent blue glass.

"How do you feel?" I asked, as I stood by the door waiting to be asked inside.

"My fever came as usual, but it didn't stay so long. I feel much better, stronger, but you can't examine me until I am cleaned up and the sheets are changed. Come back at ten. But it is nice to see you so early. I expected you on the second train."

She looked remarkably better to me.

"I guess Dr. Jacquet's treatment is beginning to work," she said with a smile.

"Then a little later I will return," I said.

As I closed the door behind me, I bumped into the morning nurse, who said sarcastically, "You might as well have stayed over."

I felt my face turn crimson as I scurried away to see Madame Fabron. Two women carrying the same illness, the older one in stable condition and the younger one desperately ill. That was the instructor's intent: to demonstrate the range of TB in 1952.

Madame Fabron was in her chair where I had left her the day before.

"Good morning, Doctor," she said. "You are an early riser. That is good; it shows a strong character and devotion. I, too, have been up early. I have already taken my morning walk. Last night I slept on my balcony for two hours in the cold air, which was invigorating. Did you ever read Boccaccio, Doctor, *The Nightingale?* You should. Then you could understand how I felt last night outside."

"Does Dr. Jacquet include champagne in his treatment program?" I asked.

"No, but he believes if the mind is well, then cure

is inevitable, and if a glass or two of champagne makes patients happy, he allows it. The professor believes the TB bacilli do not like good champagne, but the brain does. Do you know his theory, why people catch TB?"

"I don't," I said. "He has not lectured to us yet. Actually, I haven't even met him."

"Oh, you will. If you don't meet him, I will introduce you. He is a remarkable man. Not only is he a great doctor, but he is a major in the Swiss army. Now, to his theory: he believes people who have had terrible disappointments and who suffer from melancholy will develop TB or other diseases.

"My illness started when I was a young woman living at the palace—where I worked as a private secretary to the sultan. My husband took up with the governess and ran away with her, leaving me with a six-year-old child. I became so depressed that I planned to kill myself. At the palace they tried all sorts of potions and hydrobath cures. They soaked me in ice water and then put me into a steaming bath. The doctor of the palace was convinced that I had to be isolated, so they placed me in a cell-like room and fed me nothing but water and vitamins. I began to lose weight but remained dreadfully depressed. As I was all alone in the prime of my youth with no man, the wise man concluded it was necessary for me to have an operation to remove the excitable part of my body. They removed my clitoris with one quick swipe of the razor as they administered ether."

"Where was this done?" I asked in disbelief.

"In the palace there was a women's clinic for deliveries and other operations."

I remembered reading that certain parts of the world

practiced this barbaric ritual. It's even more incredible that these mutilations are still taking place today.

"But this, too, did not cure my depression. And when I began to lose more weight and develop night sweats and started to cough blood, they diagnosed me as having tuber-culosis and sent me here to Leysin twenty-five years ago. As in so many famous stories, I became ill because of my misfortunes."

I wasn't convinced, and I'm still not, that an illness can be caused or cured by the state of the mind alone. It is cured by a brilliant, marvelous drug that kills the bacilli. Antibiotics for TB, when they were discovered, closed all the sanatori-ums in a few years. So it is with every illness.

The nurse arrived an hour later and I examined Madame Fabron's lungs, heart, and stomach. I found no abnormalities.

"Well, Doctor—or what should I call a second-year med-ical student? You found nothing. I am glad; it means I am getting better."

I went to the the X-ray department and found Madame Fabron's most recent films. I brought them into the office of a Russian radiologist, who was sipping coffee and smoking a cigarette.

"We haven't taken a film from Madame Fabron in years," he said. "She refuses to be X-rayed. This one was taken five years ago."

We both looked at her films—he with his expert eye and I as a novice.

"Are you sure these are her films?" he asked.

"This is what they gave me."

"According to these films, she no longer has active TB," he said. "In essence, she is cured. We normally perform

X-rays on the patients every six months, so there must be earlier films on file."

We looked through the old files and located her chest films from ten years earlier, which did demonstrate the classic TB signs of a large hole or cavity in the lung.

"How does she feel?" the radiologist asked.

"She complains of fatigue, but I did not find anything on examination."

"Well, then, ask the doctor in charge of her case to order some sputum collections. According to the number of TB in the sputum, the TB is classified as to its infectability, from 1 to 4, and in a contagious stage, extra precautions are taken by the staff."

But I had seen no signs of anyone taking precautions, such as wearing masks and gloves when examining any of the patients. Most of the doctors who stayed at Leysin developed a positive test for TB, meaning that they had contracted a mild form of it. Just what was going on here?

It was eleven o'clock in the morning when I returned to see Madame Fabron. The sun still had not broken through the clouds, and the mountains were not visible. There was that dampness in the air before it begins to snow. She was sitting on her chaise longue on the balcony, wearing sunglasses.

"The lights up here are so strong," she said, "that they hurt my eyes." She was wearing a Persian lamb coat and a Persian hat, looking like a Russian princess riding on a sled.

"I am sorry to bother you again," I said, "but I need to ask you some more questions before I write up your report."

"You are very serious. Relax a little, young man. You will be all worn out before you are thirty. But go on, ask me your questions.

"I asked Madame Fabron the same questions I had already posed to her.

"As I told you, Doctor, I am only tired, and if I do just what the doctor tells me, I get by each day. It is almost lunchtime. Can I offer you a glass of Moët?"

I declined her offer and went to see Dr. Duvalle, her doctor. When I asked about collecting sputum from Madame Fabron, he gave me an annoyed look and said, "When you write your report, include that as part of the suggestions."

"But would it not be better if I had the sputum results so I could write a thorough report, including the prognosis?"

"Your 'stage' will be finished in a week or so, and it takes several months for the culture. Unless, of course, you would like to stay here for the rest of the semester and wait for the cultures to return? And by the way, it is not necessary for you to arrive here at seven in the morning unless you want to help the kitchen to prepare breakfast."

As a student and young doctor, I would be meeting many more doctors like him. I could never understand how such insensitive people could work with patients. But when one of the patients strolled past Dr. Duvalle, he transformed into a different person, remarkably charming and warm.

After lunch I went out onto the large terrace, which resembled the deck of a luxury ocean liner. There was no sun, and the sky was covered with great ominous clouds. I was shivering from the damp air, but the patients were lying on chaises longues, barely dressed, taking their outdoor cure.

Gabrielle was on one of those chairs, covered with a light sheet, still reading her book of poetry. For a few minutes I watched her from a distance. Her long brown hair fell to her shoulders, and her face had a peaceful look. Occasionally she looked up, giving a pleasant greeting to a passerby.

"Hello, Gabrielle," I said as I approached. "Aren't you cold?"

"A little, but I get used to it. Dr. Jacquet said it is the best thing for me. I missed you this morning. I was all cleaned up, waiting for you to examine me."

"I know, I am sorry. I had to see another patient."

"Was she pretty?"

"Yes, but not as pretty as you. She is old enough to be your grandmother," I said.

"Pull a chair over and sit a little while with me. Then we can go in, and you can examine me. You are wearing a different tie today," she said.

I had just grabbed any tie that morning, rushing out to catch the train. I tried to suppress my pleasure that she had noticed it.

"You are as old as I am, I bet," she said.

"Just about; perhaps a year or two older."

"Do you have a girlfriend in America?"

"No."

"How about here in Lausanne?"

"No, Gabrielle. I have no girlfriends. I am too busy to find a girlfriend."

"You are a cute-looking guy. I bet there are plenty of girls who would like to go out with an American medical student."

"Well, I have not met them yet."

"Do you like to dance?"

"No, I don't know how to very well."

"I could teach you when I get better. I would like to dance for you."

"I would be honored, Gabrielle."

"It will take me a long time to get back into shape. Ballet is really hard work." She moved her small body under the sheet as if she were standing by an exercise barre in front of a mirror.

"I dance Petrouchka the best, and Swan Lake. Have you ever seen a ballet?"

"Yes, I saw Swan Lake in New York, and the Nutcracker Suite."

"I was invited to the MetropoLana'sn Ballet School for one year, but then I became ill," she said softly. Her eyes grew moist, and I felt a sick feeling in the pit of my stomach.

"Can you take me back to my room?" she asked. "I am getting chilled. I think the fever is coming back."

I wheeled her back to the room under the suspicious eyes of the other patients.

"Now, if the other doctors were only as thoughtful," teased the nurse from that morning, "it would make our work easier."

"Can you help me? I need to examine Gabrielle now."

"It is not necessary," Gabrielle said.

"It is a hospital rule, Gabrielle," the nurse explained. "No doctor examines a female patient without a nurse—especially young, handsome, male medical students."

Nurse Maria was a large woman who reminded me of the actress Simone Signoret. It was obvious she cared a great deal about the gentle Gabrielle, not only as a patient but as if she were her daughter.

I waited outside the door as Gabrielle was undressed and made ready for the examination. "Come on in, doctor of the future," I heard Nurse Maria yell. "I just took her temperature for you, Doctor, and it is normal for the first time in weeks. You bring good luck to Gabrielle."

I looked into her mouth first and found her tonsils to be small, but not infected. I examined her tiny ears with an otoscope, and I could hear her breathing close to my ear. Nurse Maria undid her hospital gown and held it in front of her chest as I proceeded to examine her lungs. I tapped the back of her chest to find areas of dullness and areas that would sound like a drum if there were a cavity underneath my hand. I could not find any of these abnormalities until Gabrielle said, "You have to go higher. That is where my cavity lies. Here," she said, and twisted her hand in back, touching my hand.

She was right. The tapping sound changed dramatically to a sound like a drummer playing. With my hand flat on her chest, I asked her to whisper "thirty-three." No doctors perform this exercise anymore, but in those days we were taught in medical school that the particular reverberation when a patient uttered that number revealed whether the lungs were filled with fluid or contained a cavity. My stethoscope on her chest moved slowly each inch as I heard both lungs wheeze and rattle and gurgle like a sulfur geyser I had once heard on a volcanic mountain. I moved to the front of her chest and Nurse Maria dropped the sheet, revealing her youthful body. Gabrielle's face flushed, and she closed her eyes as I listened to her heart.

In the old days, doctors placed their ears directly on a patient's chest. Besides causing embarrassment for female patients, there was also a real fear of catching fleas from patients, which was what prompted the great French clinician René Laennec to invent the stethoscope in 1816.

In Leysin the older doctors, on occasion, still placed an ear directly on a patient's chest to better hear the sounds of the heart and lungs.

The front of Gabrielle's chest was wheezing as loudly as the back, and her heart was racing. Her eyes opened, and she looked directly at me as I listened to her heart under her breast. I felt my face turn beet red and swiftly moved away as Nurse Maria covered up her moist chest.

She started to wheeze more than ever, and Nurse Maria asked me, "Do you make all your patients wheeze?"

"Only if they are allergic to me," I replied.

"Very clever, Doctor."

Gabrielle was now lying on the pillow. Her face had turned a purple-red, but her wheezing had subsided to some degree.

"I am very sick, am I not?" she asked with a sad, desperate voice.

"Not so sick, Gabrielle. I have seen others who are much sicker get better and cured."

"You better learn to lie so it doesn't show on your face, because no patient will believe what you say," she said.

"Look, Gabrielle, I am only a medical student. You are my second case of TB. You ask me questions like I was some kind of expert. I really don't know how sick you are."

"Don't get annoyed. I was only trying to get information."

"I am not annoyed, just frustrated."

"Well, then, you need a girlfriend."

Nurse Maria gleamed with pleasure as we carried on this way, then reminded me that the last train was leaving in minutes.

"Are you coming early again tomorrow, before the rest of

the students?" Gabrielle asked.

"Of course I am. I have to look at your X ray and write up your report and that of my other patient. Have a good evening."

"I will miss you until tomorrow."

I wanted to tell her that I would miss her, too, but I dared not. I never dropped my professional demeanor, but I was treading close to a line that was crossed more commonly in earlier eras than it is today, when doctors spend far less time with patients and are rarely alone with patients of the opposite sex.

Nurse Maria accompanied me down the long hall and said, "You did very well. She is very sick, the poor sweetheart, and she cares a lot for you."

"And I for her,"' I said.

"How much longer will you be with us?"

"A few more days," I told her.

"Don't tell her unless she asks. She has no friends here and does not get many visitors, except once a month her parents come. She is so young and beautiful," the nurse continued, "and she is a dreamer. She resents the doctors and all the people who can come and go freely. I am always afraid she will do something foolish."

"Like what?" I asked in panic.

"Like leaving her bed at night and walking to the edge of the terrace and throwing herself down the mountain."

"But that can't happen! She has to be watched all the time."

"That is not possible," Nurse Maria explained.

"Have any patients ever done such a thing?"

"Yes, but usually the older ones."

Back in the city that night, I wrote up a ten-page report on Madame Fabron, concluding that she no longer had active TB and could be discharged from the sanatorium. The whole time my thoughts were of Gabrielle.

The following morning I chose a bright red tie and blue shirt and took extra time to comb my hair. I brought a bouquet of white flowers for Gabrielle. The sky was cold and gray when I arrived at the top of the mountain. This morning the hospital looked deserted. Then I realized it was Saturday and most of the students and staff would be off until Monday morning.

Gabrielle was sleeping peacefully, looking angelic. Beads of perspiration dotted her white forehead. Sleep is a blessing for the sick; it is the only refuge they have.

Dr. Duvalle greeted me coldly as I arrived on Ward B. "I finished my report on Madame Fabron," I told him.

"That is very good. Leave it on my desk and I will grade it and return it to you on Monday. What is your conclusion?" he asked.

"I think she no longer has active TB."

"You are likely correct. Why don't you tell her the good news? She will be most grateful to you, and then she can leave and Dr. Jacquet can chalk up another cure."

Madame Fabron was sipping from a small cup when I arrived at her room.

"Will you have some real Turkish coffee?" she asked. "On Saturday, I treat myself with this luxury. You are an enthusiastic young man. Have you come to examine me?"

"No, I came to tell you some great news."

"I always like to hear good news. What is it?"

"You no longer have TB! You can leave the sanatorium."

"Are you sure?"

"Well, I think so. Dr. Duvalle agrees. I wanted to tell you right away. I was so excited."

She quietly sipped her coffee.

"Where is your report?" she asked. "I'd like to see it."

"It is in Dr. Duvalle's office."

She slowly stood up from her chair, faced the icon on her night table, and placed her hands together as if to pray. "You fool," she started quietly, and then began to scream. "This is my home. I can't leave here! Where will I go? I have no home. I have been here for twenty-five years, and you tell me I am cured. How dare you! Dr. Jacquet knows I am still sick. I can't leave here until I die!" she screamed. Then she began to sob as I had never heard a person cry, desperate, howling sobs.

Dr. Duvalle had heard the screaming and was at the door when I left.

"What happened in there?" he asked. He saw my pale face and smirked with delight.

"I told her she was cured. Why didn't you tell me I shouldn't?"

"You didn't ask."

"You knew all this time she did not have to be here?"

"Yes. We sort of let her stay here and go along with her madness, but now it will have to change."

"Why?"

"Because she will have to come to our weekly conference about which patients can be discharged. You will be back in Lausanne completing your studies and get a wonderful recommendation for your thorough work, and she will be out on the street."

"But that's terrible. And why blame it on me? You

assigned me to the case."

"Unless, of course, you want to withdraw your report, and you will get an incomplete."

"I am not going to hold back the truth!" I yelled at him.

"That is your choice, sir."

Madame Fabron was permitted to remain at the sanatorium until it closed when most of the patients were cured.

The radiologist on call for the weekend was well acquainted with Gabrielle's illness. He retrieved her X-ray films, and in the darkness of the room uttered a sad sigh.

"If you look here, she has two large TB cavities which are not healing. That corresponds to your physical findings," he said. "We collapsed the lung once, called a pneumothorax, which did nothing to help her. Medical treatment is a continual game of hits and misses; luckily most patients get better despite their treatment."

He saw the forlorn look on my face even in the darkness of the X-ray room.

"So you think she will die?" I asked.

"I am just a radiologist. I deal in shadows. That is the question you have to address to Dr. Jacquet when he returns. Some patients live on for months, others for weeks, and then there is always the chance a cure for TB will be developed. They are not too far from it now. There is a doctor by the name of Waxman, in Boston, who has been working on a drug. You have a special interest in this case?" he asked me.

"I care a lot for Gabrielle. She is too young to die."

"We all do. She is as gentle as an edelweiss flower on our mountains. But her sputum is swarming with active TB," the radiologist continued. "She also has a heart murmur that has developed since she's been in the hospital."

"A heart murmur? I did not hear one, and I examined her just yesterday."

"It is not easy to hear. One of our interns picked it up, and the cardiologist confirmed it. That is another one of her problems we have to solve."

Was I causing more harm than good here? First I caused great chaos in Madame Fabron's life, and now I had missed something as serious as a heart murmur.

"Don't look so downcast," the radiologist said. "Go and listen to her heart again and you will hear it. That is why you go to medical school—to learn! This won't be the only time you will miss a heart murmur. Why do you think I became a radiologist?" he laughed. He placed his arm about my shoulder and said, "You can only become a doctor if you care and if you experience failure. It makes you humble and more careful."

I found Gabrielle sitting up in a chair by the window in her room, her hair tied in a ponytail with a small red ribbon. "Thank you for the paper narcissus. They are beautiful."

"How are you feeling?"

"Better, but a little sad. Look outside." The entire world was white, the mountains no longer visible and the last few red autumn leaves off the trees. It was snowing heavily.

"Snow comes early to Leysin and never leaves," she said. "Dr. Jacquet makes us lie out on the snow when the sun is out with only our underclothing on."

"Gabrielle, I have to listen to your heart again."

"How nice. You know it makes me a little nervous, but only when you examine me. I love your bedside manners. You are so gentle."

"I am going to call the nurse. I will be right back."

"You don't have to call the nurse. I trust you."

"I'd rather call the nurse, Gabrielle."

Luckily Nurse Maria was working that weekend. She was sitting at her desk, busy writing in the charts.

"I am sorry to bother you, but could you help me again? I have to listen to Gabrielle's heart."

"You did that yesterday."

"I know, but apparently I missed a heart murmur. I can't write the report up until I hear it."

"It is Saturday. All the students are gone. Why don't you go back to Lausanne? Come back on Monday. I am the only nurse on for two wings." She looked at me again. "When you get that puppy look on your face," she said, "you and that little ballerina I can't resist! All right, come on. You have ten minutes."

"I need five."

This time I listened to Gabrielle's heart first while she was sitting up and then again lying down, and I detected the murmur. It came from one of the valves of the heart, but I was not certain which one.

"Why are you listening so much? Do I have heart trouble now? If I do, it is all your fault."

"Thank you, Nurse Marais," I said.

"Will you be back today?" Gabrielle asked.

"Yes, but I have to write up your case before I forget everything."

The sanatorium had a large comfortable library with easy chairs, tables, and good lighting. I sat there and described my findings in detail. I was troubled because my only diagnosis was pulmonary TB; I was left without an explanation for the cause of the heart murmur.

It was past five p.m. when I finally finished the long write-up, and it was dark outside. The snow fell furiously, the wind howling in circles around the sanatorium.

When I returned to Gabrielle's room, the nurse told me the trains had been shut down for the night.

"Oh, wonderful. Then you will have to stay here all night. Thank you, storm," Gabrielle said.

"I suppose you will want to eat here with the princess," the nurse said.

With not much resolution I said, "I will eat in the cafeteria."

"Nonsense! I will bring you a tray, too," Nurse Maria told me, "and perhaps I can sniff around and find a carafe of wine. You worked hard today and you deserve it. But don't go shouting this to the other students!"

Half an hour later, Nurse Maria returned with two trays, a small white tablecloth, two candles, and a carafe of red wine.

"There now, *ma petite, bon appétit.*" She returned minutes later with a blanket and a pillow "in case you decide to sleep on the chair next to mademoiselle."

There was a small radio in the room and Edith Piaf was singing, *"Mon Homme."* My Man.

"Do you like the Little Bird, too?" Gabrielle asked.

"She is my favorite singer," I replied.

I lit the two small candles on the round table and ate the usually unappetizing hospital meal, which tonight was like a feast. The candlelight's glow made Gabrielle's face appear languid and beautiful. For dessert we had small pieces of ripened Camembert while sipping wine. Gabrielle's face turned red. At first I thought it was from the wine, but it was her night temperature rising. She tried to suppress a cough, and then her wheezing became audible. She rose from the table and opened the drab-looking blinds.

"I have to open the window just a bit. It helps me breathe better."

Snowflakes settled on her brown hair as they sped through the window. She took a swallow of the purple medicine by her bedside and the wheezing began to subside. From her dresser she brought out some photographs of herself and placed them on the table, like a fortuneteller.

"Perhaps it will be the worst snowstorm of the century and you will have to stay here for days with me," she said. "Would you like that?"

"Yes, I would like that very much."

A doctor cannot fall in love with a patient, but it happens anyway.

"These are my parents in front of our house, and my two sisters."

"They all look like you," I remarked, "but not as pretty."

"Do you think I am pretty?"

"Of course, very."

"Much prettier than any of your girlfriends?"

"Yes, if I had any girlfriends."

"Then you really like me?"

"Yes, of course I do. I like you a lot, Gabrielle."

She gave me a sweet coy smile and loosened the little ribbon that held her hair, which came falling down her back in a gentle cascade.

"This is me dancing." She produced a photograph of herself doing a pirouette, wearing her leotards. Other photographs showed Gabrielle in her Petrushka costume. She looked at the pictures with an anguished expression on her face.

"I will never dance again," she said in a solemn voice. "You saw my X-rays, did you not?"

"Yes."

"Well, they must be pretty bad. When do you think I will die?"

"That is ridiculous! You don't know what you are saying. If you are going to talk like that, I am going to leave."

She started to cry. I wanted to cry with her. I sat next to her and placed my arms around her small soft shoulders.

"You will be cured in a few months, Gabrielle, and you won't even remember this place when you get back on the stage."

"Are you sure? I will believe you for tonight. Because tonight is a magical night. I feel so alive for the first time since I came to Leysin. God sent the snow to keep you here for me. I want to dance for you."

"I want to see you dance, which will be very soon."

"Not very soon. Now. Tonight. I feel strong enough. You step outside and I will put on my leotards. Return in a few minutes. Dr. Jacquet said that some exercise is good for me."

"Gabrielle, you can't dance now. You are not strong enough. You might harm yourself." She started to undo her robe.

"All right. All right," I said, as it became clear I couldn't dissuade her. "Call when you are ready."

When I returned she was dressed in her leotards, and she looked adorable. Her hair was drawn into a bun, and she was bent over slightly with her delicate arms crossed over her side. She moved her body gracefully, with her arms stretched, circling in mid-air, and then she was on her toes circling the room, then jumping in the air. I stood entranced by the scene. For a moment we were both transported to a recital hall. Beads of perspiration appeared on her forehead as she bounced from one end of the small room to the other. Her eyes never left mine. Then she stopped, bowed her head, and knelt down as I applauded.

"Gabrielle. You are incredible. That was beautiful."

"Did you really like me?"

"I'm speechless."

She fell back on the bed, wiping her forehead with a towel.

"Now I am tired. I want to take a little rest, but you now have to read to me with your cute French accent from my poetry book. Here," she said, "read 'The Living Flame' by Baudelaire. I will close my eyes and imagine we are in a small café in Paris on the Left Bank, and we are sipping fine cognac and coffee and it is late at night."

I started to read the beautiful poem aloud. One of the lines I was fearful to recite: "They sing of Death, you sing the Resurrection....Bright stars whose brilliance no sun can dull!"

But when I looked up, Gabrielle was sleeping soundly. I covered her with a blanket and sat in the hard, uncomfortable chair, scrutinizing her labored breathing. There would be many times, I realized, when I would be sitting by the bedside of a critically ill patient. Would it always feel this excruciating? I could not imagine the world without my sweet Gabrielle.

Several hours later she awoke, uttering a soft gentle sigh, as if returning from a beautiful dream. I was still in the chair, finishing up her case history.

"You are still here while I am sleeping. I am sorry. You must be so bored."

"Actually not. I was doing my homework."

"Writing about me? I hope it is nice things." She pulled the vase of flowers from her night table and held them close to her bosom.

"These are so beautiful. No one ever gave me flowers like this. Now I know you like me a little."

She sat up and her face blushed. "I never had a man, and I am going to die, no matter what you say. Do you like me a lot?"

"Yes, you know I do."

"Do you think I am sexy? You did see me when you examined me."

"I remember."

"Well?"

"Well, what? You are a beautiful young woman."

"Do you like my body?"

"Gabby, that is not a question to ask me."

"No one has ever called me that."

"In America, you would be called Gabby."

"Will you do one thing for me tonight, because this is a special night? It was given to us."

I feared what was coming next.

"Make love to me. I just want to know how it feels. I dreamed you did. It was such a heavenly dream. No one would know, and I would not betray you. You don't have to kiss me, because my mouth is filled with deadly bacteria and I wouldn't want you to get sick. You are too sweet and dear to me."

I wanted to race to her and place my arms around her to protect her from the angel of death, but she saw the anguish on my face and began to cry.

"I'm sorry," I said, shaking my head slowly.

I did not need a Hippocratic Oath to explain to me how I had to behave at such moments. My vulnerability would be similarly tested many times during my medical career, but never would rejecting a patient's romantic interest feel this wrenching. I had never felt so deeply about anyone before.

Gabrielle cried herself to sleep while I sat motionless on the chair.

When early morning finally arrived, I crept out of the room as she remained in her peaceful sleep. The trains were running again. Outside it was still dark. It had stopped snowing and a sliver of moonlight reflected on the pure white night.

From the train I watched the sun rise over the Alps as it moved slowly through the snow-packed tracks. By the time I arrived back at my small room, I had decided that I would continue to care for Gabrielle. I would get permission to see her every weekend until she was well, no longer as a student but as her friend.

I spent Sunday in the library and then searched for a present I would give her the next day. All the stores were closed except a tobacconist, and there I found a funny-looking cowboy made of marzipan.

On Monday morning I took the five o'clock train to Leysin. My heart was pounding with anticipation of seeing my ballet dancer. I waited for the freight elevator, which once again contained a body on a stretcher pushed by two orderlies. When I arrived at Ward B there was no one on the floor.

The hall smelled of disinfectant. Gabrielle's door was open, but the only one in the room was a woman kneeling on the floor with a pail, scrubbing the floor and walls.

I raced outside and saw an older man and woman standing by the nurse's desk. I recognized them from the pictures that Gabrielle had shown me. Her parents were signing some papers and being handed a bag of clothing.

"Where is Gabrielle? What happened?"

"Gabrielle is in Heaven," the woman said, and started to cry.

"She died on Sunday," Nurse Maria said softly. "In her sleep."

I looked at her parents and felt I had known them all my life. Her mother had the same face as Gabrielle.

"Did you know my daughter?" the father asked.

"Yes, we were friends for a short time."

I had to look away when tears filled my eyes.

A short time later, streptomycin was introduced for the treatment of TB—the miracle drug that arrived too late to save Gabrielle.

A few weeks after she died, I reached into my inside jacket pocket and found the picture of her in her leotards. She must have slipped it into my pocket while I slept at her bedside. She had inscribed it, "This is how I want you to remember me," and she quoted a line from the poem we had read together: "You sing the Resurrection of my soul."

I still do.

KNOWING MEURICE
1938/1970

WHEN WE ARRIVED IN AMERICA IN 1938 FROM POLAND, we lived in a small apartment on 99th Street in Manhattan. Each day was a lesson in survival, which I have never forgotten. My father, once an important industrialist, was reduced to shoveling snow off the streets in the winter to earn a few dollars to feed us.

In the basement of our rooming house a tall, fat, ugly man ran a thriving business cleaning and pressing suits and shirts. He had a son called Meurice who, after school, delivered the shirts and pants to the neighborhood customers.

One cold day in December, when I was standing in front of the house, I met Meurice carrying suits and bundles of packaged shirts from his father's store.

He sized me up and looked at me curiously because I was wearing leather short pants (lederhosen) on this cold day.

"Why don't you wear long pants?" he asked me. I was eight years old and had been in America only two months. I had a bare knowledge of English. I did not understand a word he said, so I just smiled. That made him angry.

"Do you want a punch in your face?" he asked me. I understood that, as he raised a fist at me in annoyance. Just at that moment his father emerged from the cellar of his store wearing a stained polo shirt, a cigar stuck in his mouth, reeking from sweat and alcohol.

"Meurice!" he yelled. "Deliver those pants, damn you. He is a greenhorn. He doesn't know any English."

Meurice must have felt bad because he signaled me with his hand to accompany him on his delivery.

I followed him to a large apartment building on the corner of West End Avenue, through the servants' entrance, up the service elevator to the twelfth floor. He rang the bell. A black woman dressed in a white uniform answered the door. She took the packages, paid the bill, and gave Meurice twenty-five cents for a tip.

"See how easy it is," he said, and showed me the quarter in the palm of his hand.

The following afternoon, after school, I waited for Meurice in front of his store. When he arrived, he was carrying a pair of long pants on a hanger.

"Here, this is for you. They are the same size as mine. No one ever came to pick them up."

He took me down to his father's store for a fitting. His father was standing over a large pressing machine, a bottle of beer on the counter. The small room was suffused with the smell of alcohol and smoke as he took a swallow from the bottle, held it in his mouth, and then sprayed the beer on the pants on his pressing board. With one quick thrust, he slammed the large steam board onto the pants and was suddenly surrounded by a cloud of smoke. The pants were a perfect fit. Meurice and I became good friends thereafter.

"My father will pay twenty-five cents for each delivery," he said. "It is Christmastime and we need help."

Meurice was different from the other boys I knew. He was fair in appearance, slender, and his movements were not like the other boys'. He never played curb ball, and was quite shy and kept to himself most of the time. He hated baseball, and was not interested in any of the radio programs I learned to love. It did not take long for me to become Americanized and become a fan of The Shadow, Captain Midnight, The Green Hornet, The Lone Ranger, and all the other marvelous radio characters.

The war ended and another war started. Meurice had quit high school and moved to Greenwich Village with a friend. Occasionally he came to visit his father, who still ran his little shop. I continued to live in the same neighborhood, and Meurice came by to visit me. He was now tall, handsome, slim, and unashamed of his homosexuality. He worked as a stage set helper in a theater in the Village and had been rejected from miLana'sry service. Meurice, as a child, had feminine features and appeared fragile. Now, being tall and slim, he looked like a pale weed that a strong wind could break in half.

Twenty years passed and I had become a doctor. One day, after being interviewed on Phil Regis's show to publicize my first book, I received a phone call from a man with a feminine voice who sounded desperate. "This is Meurice, remember me?"

"Of course I do. What are you doing these days?"

"I saw you on the Regis show and I want to tell you you were terrific."

"Thank you! It's nice to hear from you."

"I have to see you. I have a medical problem that no one seems able to solve. Would you take me on as a patient?"

"Yes, of course, Meurice. I will be glad to see you."

Ominous words: "I have a problem that no one can solve." I have heard them many times. It usually means the patient has wandered from doctor to doctor, plenty of tests have been performed with no diagnosis, and there is an underlying psychiatric problem. But once in a while there is a hidden ailment that has not reared its ugly head.

Meurice had not aged a day. His pale baby face did not have one wrinkle and he did not look ill.

"You look the same," he told me, "except your hair is gray, which makes you look more distinguished, like a real doctor. You have the same strong eyes that I remember." And he suddenly burst out laughing.

"What's so funny, Meurice?"

"I just remembered how we went to the World's Fair in 1939 and we took one of those little car rails and you found a wallet on the seat and inside was fifteen dollars. We came with two dollars each and then we were rich."

"We should have given the wallet to the guard," I told Meurice.

"Well, we didn't and we went to see everything, including the girly show, the Billy Rose Aquacade, the Streets of Paris, and the parachute jump, and you had your first ice cream soda.

"But I am here for professional reasons, so I'll get to the point. For many years I have always felt weaker than most people. I become dizzy and feel weak when I stand too long, especially in a warm room, and now I have had five or more fainting spells, and I am losing weight. I have seen many doctors and they find nothing wrong with me except that my blood pressure is low, which I am told is a good sign."

Nature had played a mean trick on Meurice. When he stood naked in front of me in the examining room, his skin was pale, soft, the body hair scant. He could have easily passed for a woman. I could not find anything from the examination to account for fainting spells, or "swooning like a Victorian maiden," as Meurice put it.

As I was making notes in the chart, Meurice was getting dressed and he suddenly swayed like a drunken sailor and fell back on the examining table. His blood pressure and EKG were normal, yet he lay there unconscious. I called an ambulance and by the time it arrived, Meurice was awake.

"I am not going into the hospital because they never find anything wrong with me. It is a waste of money," he said.

As he lay on the examining table, I listened to his heart again. The beat was regular and there were no murmurs.

"Well, you are probably right, Meurice, but a few days in the hospital would be worthwhile so we can observe you and perhaps do some more tests and repeat some of the others."

"No, I will not have a hundred needle sticks and curious doctors pawing at me."

"But, according to the records you brought with you, you have not been studied in a hospital like Yale, a university hospital where someone might have a clue to your mystery."

"No, thank you."

The ambulance left without him, and I resigned myself that I could not help Meurice. Then I had a thought.

"Just one more question, Meurice," I said. "Are these spells always the same? What I mean is, do they happen usually after you have been sitting for a while and then stand up?"

"Yes, usually. Sometimes they happen after standing a long time."

"Lie down again, Meurice," I instructed.

I took his blood pressure again and it was normal. Ten minutes later he stood up, and his blood pressure did not drop significantly, but his face became pale.

"Are you sure there are no other things that are different from before?"

"Well, my joints are always aching," he said, "and I am so tired all the time. Just climbing the stairs exhausts me, and my breath is a little shorter than it used to be."

His chest X-ray was normal and Meurice did not smoke or drink.

"I'd better sit down," he said, "before I go off again."

"Wait one second more, Meurice. I just want to listen to your heart again."

I placed the stethoscope on his hairless chest and was surprised to hear a new sound in his heart. It was not a murmur, but it sounded like a bag of sand that was falling to the ground, a plopping sound with each heartbeat. He lay back on the table and the sound disappeared. He sat up, and it still was not there. But when he stood up, I heard it again, a strange, faraway sound, as if I was in an old house and it came from down in the cellar. I was certain I had discovered the mystery of my swooning friend.

At just about that time I was involved in a new procedure called echocardiography. It is a method for picturing the heart through sound waves. In 1970 the procedure was still in its infancy and we used very primitive instruments and Polaroid pictures. We were not certain what we were seeing.

Meurice was suffering from a rare tumor of the heart called a myxoma, which grows slowly. When it reaches a certain size, it impedes the flow of blood through the heart and sends out a sound like a plop when the person changes position.

"I know the diagnosis, Meurice, but it won't be easy to prove. My crude echogram did show something abnormal in the heart. You will have to come into the hospital and allow me to arrange for an angiogram of your heart, an X-ray, which we can do through a heart catheterization."

It took a great deal of cajoling, but Meurice did agree, and my suspicions were confirmed. The tumor was removed, Meurice's fainting spells vanished, and he moved to Paris to do what he always dreamed of—become a female impersonator.

Before his surgery he had been unable to stand up long enough to perform without fainting. But I was able to travel to Paris and watch him perform in a little bistro in Paris as a perfect Marlene Dietrich singing "Falling in Love Again."

SECRET
MISSION
1952

IT WAS A BLEAK TIME NOT ONLY IN AMERICA, BUT ALL OVER the world. Nuclear warheads were pointed at the U.S., and war with Russia seemed imminent. People were building bomb shelters stacked with cans of food, biscuits, candles, favorite books, and rudimentary medical supplies.

I was a struggling student at the City College of New York, attending night school and working in a factory scrubbing pieces of animal fur. I had to wear a plastic mask that still carried the imprint of the person who had worn it before me. Each morning, I arrived at 6 a.m. at the factory, located on 36th Street, between Fifth and Sixth Avenues, the fur district of New York. I changed into old gray work clothing. I was given a coarse bristle brush and a piece of fur that had to be rubbed smooth with kerosene. Each skin was then inspected by a man with a gray complexion. Without speaking, the inspector turned the animal skin over on the bench and, if satisfied, placed it on a pile where the tailor then arranged them into patterns on large tables with cutouts of necks, chests, backs, and fronts. Then, they proceeded to use special skin scissors and designed the fur strips to fit the outlines. The sewing machine operators then took over and in surprisingly little time, they had sleeves and collars, giving the shapeless pieces of fur a body.

At lunchtime I usually ate a sandwich on the fire escape and read my chemistry book. At five o'clock I'd rush to change my clothing and take the subway to 137th Street and walk up the long steep hill to the CCNY Chemistry Lab.

I loved breathing in the smell of the laboratory rather than the disgusting odor of kerosene and furs. At times, the experiments would take hours, but I did not mind leaving at 11 p.m., rushing back to the subway and home to 99th Street to take a quick shower and sleep, then start again at 6:00 a.m. I was determined to finish college and go to medical school. It took six years of grueling night school to receive my B.S. degree from CCNY, a tough school known as the Harvard of the poor.

During those turbulent years we were called "Pinkies" because we rioted against McCarthy and burned a professor in effigy because of his anti-Semitic ways (they subsequently fired him). Then came the basketball scandal. Our team performed strongest in the finals, but it turned out they were throwing some games. This wonderful tuition-free academic school that boasted top scholars and even Nobel Prize winners was disgraced.

I graduated during the Korean War and was called up to the Draft Board for a hearing. It was located on the first floor of a familiar building on 96th Street and Broadway. In the basement was a Ping-Pong parlor that had been a second home for me. Each afternoon after high school I went there with my friend and we hustled anyone who was watching. We became accomplished players and won a few tournaments, including the P.A.L. Championship.

Now here I was again, under less pleasant circumstances. The few medical schools I applied to had rejected me. Later I would figure out why: my college records were stamped with the label "Agitator" because of my protesting days.

Three austere-looking men sat with pencils and pads of paper at a table, scrutinizing me.

"Why don't you want to go into the army?" one of the more hard-nosed men with a face like a boxer asked me.

"I can be more useful to this country as a doctor," I stated. "I have arranged from a friend of mine in France to get admitted to the Sorbonne University in Toulouse to study medicine."

"All right, we will give you a deferment so you can get a medical degree," the man said. "Do you speak German and Polish?"

"Yes," I answered, "mostly German."

"But first our government would like you to help us. We will give you free passage on a cargo ship to Europe. You will go as a pharmacist's mate. We want you to deliver a briefcase to London. And there may be other assignments. Do you agree?"

"Of course. It sounds easy enough."

I didn't give a damn if this mission would be dangerous. It could not be worse than being sent to Korea.

"You will be working for an export company and a carrier called Marine State. The person who will contact you is Judge Frieda."

The next day I took a taxicab with my parents and Judge Frieda, the alleged owner of the export company, to the Brooklyn Navy Yard. When we arrived on the dock he wished me bon voyage and handed me a leather briefcase. We passed through security gates after the judge presented some papers. My mother and father were reassured that all would be well, and I dragged my suitcase and the briefcase to the bow of the ship.

There was no gangplank to walk up, just a long rope ladder. On the top deck I saw dozens of faces peering down on me. It was a late afternoon in October, and the wind was blowing from the water, causing the rope ladder to sway. One of the men from the top threw down a long rope. Another sailor standing next to me took the rope and attached it to my luggage handle as I watched my luggage, my only possessions, dangling in the air and being hoisted up. Screams and a loud roar shattered the autumn afternoon, as the sailor motioned to me by pushing out his hands and directing me to the climb Jacob's ladder.

"No!" I yelled.

"*Sim!*" he yelled, Portuguese for "yes."

"Get going," another voice yelled from the top deck. "We have been waiting for you, so start climbing and hold on."

Both voices came from harsh, weary faces, decidedly not the kind I had seen in movies and paintings as being weathered and tanned from the sea. I clutched the rope ladder and began to climb. My hand began to cramp, but if I let go I would have landed on the concrete walk below. With great concentration I managed to make it onboard.

That month there had been brutal storms and many cargo ships were wrecked. From the pilot's room one night I watched the baseboard and saw the angle of inclination at 40 degrees. Captain Ripchen explained to me that if the angle reached 60 degrees, we would be in trouble.

The following day, after dinner, I explored the ship. In one room I saw the crew playing cards at a long table. The room reeked of smoke and the men had placed large knives conspicuously on the table. I continued past swiftly.

It was still dark outside when someone banged on my cabin door. There, standing by the entrance, were two tall men wearing black raincoats, leather boots, and large leather hats.

"Police!" one announced in a loud German accent reminiscent of the Gestapo, reminding me of my family's horrifying escape from Danzig. But they were only customs officers.

We landed in Bremerhaven, Germany, and once they inspected my passport they smiled and said, "Americano from New York."

I traveled to Victoria Station in London and took a taxi to the Marine State Office, where I turned the briefcase over to the secretary. It was locked, of course. I did try to open it aboard ship but was unable to. I imagined all sorts of intrigues and thought of Graham Green stories. But why not send the documents by mail or diplomatic pouch? Why use me as courier? This was not going to be the only trip; several more would to follow.

But first I took the train to Paris to visit my uncle, before going on to the university in Toulouse, where another adventure awaited me.

LA FEMME
A LA PORTE
1951

WE WERE A SMALL GROUP OF AMERICAN OUTCASTS, unwanted by our American medical schools. We lived in the Hotel Henri in Toulouse, France.

I had graduated from CCNY and was labeled a radical and a Communist because I had participated in the riots in our school to oust an overtly anti-Semitic professor. The McCarthy years produced hosts of casualties, but for me they ushered in an exciting opportunity.

Our hotel was small, located one block from the Place Capital, the center of the city, run with a warm hand by a gracious concierge and his wife. They lived in an apartment on the ground floor, immediately behind the circular desk of the lobby.

The least expensive rooms were small, but opened on an enclosed central court with a large circular skylight. I lived, uncomfortably, in one of these rooms. It had a sink, a bed, a large armoire with a full-size mirror, and a small desk. Like all the other students, I had a miniature kerosene burner on which to brew coffee, fry eggs, and cook hamburgers in a cast iron pan. Given the inexpensive French bread, cheeses, and wine, I made do on seventy dollars a month.

I covered the walls of this tiny room, and even the

ceiling, with blackboards that I filled with formulas and detailed drawings of nerve connections for my anatomy class. I wanted to be surrounded by their names and images so they would become as much a part of me as my arms and legs. The first thing I saw when I awoke each morning was the arterial supply of the stomach, which spread across part of my ceiling. This room became my sanctuary—at once my library, dining room, sleeping quarters, and a place to dream of someday becoming a doctor.

Every day a small elderly woman came to make the beds and sweep as best she could, especially the multicolored chalk dust that covered the room and intermingled with the odors of fried food, wine, and tobacco smoke from the night before. There was one large, stained bathtub for each floor, for which we had to make reservations two days in advance. Weekends were the hardest to get. My room was moderately heated but the bathtub room was like a sauna.

Most of the students were considerably better off than I financially, and they frequently took their meals at one of the numerous nearby restaurants that served inexpensive and delicious food. My compatriots staying at the hotel included two women on Fulbright scholarships who had come to learn French culture; a medical student from St. Croix; a man from Brooklyn named Rosenberg; and Lionel Williams, also from New York.

Rosenberg spoke French fluently because this was his second year in Toulouse, preparing to retake the tests he had flunked. When he opened his room shutters, I could see a line of dried kosher salamis hanging in his open armoire. Each week they arrived, much like the newspapers, promptly and without fail. Bringing salamis to France is like bringing tea to England. How could the local food have been improved upon? Rosenberg's room looked and smelled like a New York delicatessen when he fried his treasured salamis on his kerosene stove.

You could always tell Ralph, the St. Croix native, was near by his cough. It echoed throughout the night because he kept his shutters opened. A mild and gentle man, he also spoke French fluently and was in his second year in Toulouse, having flunked his exams as well. He always had a cigarette in his hand, holding it like Peter Lorre in Casablanca, between his thumb and index finger, raising his hand, palm up, to meet his lips whenever he took a puff.

The oldest of the group was Lionel, who had a wife and two children back in Harlem. All his life he had wanted to become a doctor. His children were grown, and his wife worked hard and sent him money to enable him to pursue his dream. It was his first month here and he knew little, if any, French. He had been away from school for more than twenty years. Heavyset and tall, with a shiny brown face and a warm smile, Lionel was affable. He and I quickly became friends.

Whenever he cooked meatballs and spaghetti, he would share his meal with me. In the mornings, we left together for the bus at the Place Esquirole, which would take us to our destination and hopes: the ancient Toulouse medical school, with its long marble staircases and the anatomy laboratory, which dated back centuries.

In November, after two months at the school, the time came to dissect human bodies. We came into the lab to see twelve rectangular slabs covered with gray corpses. At first Lionel and I gasped with astonishment to see so many dead, and I could tell he was disturbed at the thought that they were about to be mutilated. Lionel was a deeply religious man. Each night before going to bed he read the Bible. Now, as he stood petrified, I saw him offer a silent prayer.

We were assigned to the same corpse—an Algerian who had died of gunshot wounds. There was an even hole in the center of his head, another in the chest. In all, four students were assigned to each corpse. Lionel and I were to start on the leg. We could not understand the instructions the professor raced through in French. A young assistant who spoke a little English gave us some basic directions about how to proceed with this ghastly business. The dissection kits were old and rusty. In college we had better tools for our frog and cat dissections. I held the scalpel in my hand, pointing at the skin. And then, for a second, I recalled the words of Macbeth: "Is this a dagger which I see before me / The handle toward my hand? Come, let me clutch thee / I have thee not, and yet I see thee still."

The incision was made; the skin of the thigh was tough and resilient, as hard as leather. Fluid oozed out. The strong smell of formaldehyde made my eyes smart and tear. It is a smell I will never forget. These were old bodies, long frozen in the morgue. When they were thawed out, life came crawling out of the legs: millions of maggots swimming in the juices of decay. I felt faint, but the pungent odor somehow kept me from swooning.

"Clean the skin area and identify the arteries and nerves and carefully dissect them clean. Cut the main artery or nerve and you fail the course before it begins."

Those were the discomfiting words of Professor Rouvière, a tall, threatening-looking man with black hair pasted down on his head. The other students at our table, Algerians and Frenchmen, knew no English. I marveled at how adroitly they performed their task. Surely they were destined to be surgeons. How cool they seemed, while Lionel and I perspired. All of us wore heavy rubber aprons. The two standing next to us were so confident that they seemed almost indifferent to what they were doing. How could anyone be indifferent to human flesh? Hadn't a corpse once been alive? What did the man do, what was he like? Now there was no name. He was Number 36660, male.

I watched the despair in Lionel's eyes. He was the same age as the corpse, the remains of a man who was now nothing more than a harbor and restaurant for maggots and an instrument of learning. I wondered, and not for the first time, if this was the right profession for me. Carefully, we moved the fat to one side and, finding the long gray nerve, began to clean it. Pull too hard, allow the slimy scalpel to slip, and that slender thread would be sliced through.

When we left in the darkness of night, our bodies reeked with the smell of death, especially our hands. Once back in my room I stripped off the offensive clothing, only to remember that there would be no washing machine, no bath to soak in. These clothes would remain my uniform. I'd have to live with the stench until I could bring them to the laundry.

Sitting at my desk, the anatomy text spread before me, I began the tedious task of translating into English; then came the memorization. Thousands of pages to memorize for just one course, and then all those others to follow—and all in French! Small wonder most flunked the exams the first time. How did anyone pass?

Becoming increasingly despondent, surrounded by the smells that brought me near to retching, I heard a gentle knock on a door. So many sounds came from that busy courtyard that I wasn't sure if the knock was intended for me. This time of night it could only be Lionel bringing me a cup of tea, as he sometimes did. Then we would sit and talk about New York and his family, and his eyes would become moist. He was terribly lonely that first month. The knock came again, more insistent, and I knew it was not Lionel.

Standing there was an apparition, a vision. My first thought was that the fumes of the formaldehyde must have gone to my head. Before me stood the most beautiful woman

I had ever seen. She was sleek and bright-eyed, vivacious and animated. She spoke first, as she saw the astonished look on my face. She must have detected the stench of formaldehyde, I thought, but she didn't refer to it.

"I saw your light on," she said in French. "Do you smoke?" she asked in English, her accent totally delightful.

"Yes. Please come in."

The only chair in the room was covered with clothing. I stuffed the clothes into the drawers of the armoire and, rummaging around in there, found a pack of matches and handed them to her.

"You are an artist," she giggled, looking up at the ceiling covered with anatomical drawings.

"No, I am a medical student."

"Yes, I heard you were the new one in the hotel."

Her perfume mingled with and then overcame the acrid smell.

"My name is Monique," she said, tilting her beautiful head slightly to the side. Her hair was brown and short, almost like a young boy's. She touched the side of her head and I saw that her fingernails were covered with a deep red polish.

"You are still studying," she said, "and it is so late. I will leave you to your work."

"No, no. I have had enough for tonight," I blurted. "Please."

I closed the door behind her and she came over to my desk and peered at the anatomy text.

"It is all in French," she said. "Do you read French, *un peu*, a little? I can help you, if you wish, in the evenings when you are back from your classes."

This was surely a dream.

Her body was small, slender, a perfect match for her delicate head and arms. Unselfconscious, she sat on the unmade bed, sniffling. After a moment she rose, walked to the desk where I was sitting, and leaned over me to peer at the book I held.

"That is the *cuisse,* how you say?"

"'Thigh.' *Voilà,* 'thigh.' It is not pretty without the skin."

She laughed seductively, and I became weak.

"I will come tomorrow again, and I will help you translate."

"You don't have to go."

"Oh *oui,* it is late and I must get my beauty sleep." She kissed me on the cheek and left the room. For the rest of the night the room was filled with her perfume and I was filled with thoughts of her.

In Europe in those days, university students were an elite group, almost always forgiven for their wild ways. If they got drunk, the Toulousian would say, "Oh, *c'est un étudiant,* they are students, what do you expect?"

You could always tell a student in Europe in the fifties. Most were unshaven or bearded, wearing old worn clothing. There was an air of freedom about them. No one was required to attend classes; all the learning was up to the student. There were no guides, no rules, only the final exams, the brutal task that always lay ahead, never for an instant out of mind. I knew that some stayed for several years trying to pass that first year's exams.

American students were even more special because of our reputation, often accurate, of being rich. I was an exception to the rule, and no one would quite believe I had barely enough money to eat one meal a day. It was almost impossible to have any social life without cash. I was prepared to lead a life of loneliness and celibacy and to concentrate all my energies on preparing for the exams.

The second home for the students was the café, a welcome reprieve from their small, dingy, usually cold and poorly lit rooms. I went as often as I could and sometimes nursed a cup of coffee undisturbed for hours. Here I heard French being spoken and watched, with great envy, love at work. The smoke-filled cafés brimmed with students animatedly speaking and laughing. Then, when it seemed hopeless that I would meet anyone, I would walk through the foggy night back to my dreary hotel. I carried a sweet melancholy in my soul.

All around me there was love. Even Rosenberg, the salami king, managed to have a girlfriend. This hotel had walls so thin that all the sounds of the night entered our rooms. Ralph coughed all night, and Rosenberg's carnal grunts pervaded the court like a bad porno movie.

At five in the morning, most of the students would have begun studying and would continue until it was time to catch the bus at eight.

Lionel was at my door at five-thirty, grinning affably.

"You had a guest at one a.m.," he said.

"Well, yes, a dream floated into my room," I told him.

For the rest of the day my thoughts were of Monique. At the lecture hall we sat on marble steps as the professor lectured with no notes while he drew the anatomy of the leg, using different colored chalks, one in each hand, to sketch in the arteries and the nerves.

"Gentlemen, that is how you must know each inch of the body."

Lionel was struggling to catch some of the words the professor spoke. Toulousians speak a special French, a wonderfully musical version. They also roll their r's, making it sound a bit like Italian.

With little sleep and distracted by my fantasy of Monique, I did not hear much of the lecture. But in the anatomy laboratory and at our post by the leg of the corpse, there was no time to daydream. Lionel struggled fiercely with his dissection. I could see the frustration line his face.

Afterward we sat in the café sipping coffee.

"It is awfully hard for me," Lionel said. "I try to remember just a little, but my head is like a sieve. Everything falls out. I can hardly understand a word, much less memorize it all."

"Lionel, it will come. Tonight you and I will review the leg and then we'll go over the biochemistry, which I think I can manage to understand."

Lionel and I went back to the hotel and worked until eleven, but it became unhappily apparent to me that he was simply not going to master the voluminous material. In his forties, his concentration was earnest but ineffective. He looked so tired when he left my room that it broke my heart.

We had eight months in which to learn all of the anatomy—10,000 pages of memorization—and five other subjects before the examination in April. All in French.

At the stroke of midnight I heard a gentle knock on the door. Monique was there, dangling an unlit cigarette in her wondrously feminine hand.

"I have come to help you. You are not too tired?"

"I have been hoping you would come. I was going to knock on your door if you didn't."

Monique lived two rooms down the hall. The shutters of her room were always tightly shut, but soft music wafted through the door, as did hints of her intoxicating perfume.

All over the bed and the chairs and the entire room, I had sprinkled Old Spice after-shave, hoping to hide the smell of formaldehyde or at least blunt its sharpness.

We sat by the desk, she moving her delicate fingers over the page, translating the complicated language of medicine, occasionally pausing to turn her seductive brown eyes toward me with a smile. By one in the morning I could no longer restrain myself, and I kissed her cheek gently.

"*Mais, non.* You have to study, *chéri,*" she reprimanded. "You are a poor student, aren't you? Not like the others?"

"Yes, but why do you ask?"

"*Comme ça,* like that."

She rose and disappeared again. I began to wonder if I had invented her. I would steal past her room every night hoping to come across her. But no sound came from the room, no light from under her door. Sometimes I knocked softly, knowing that the echo carried throughout the court. It was like announcing that I was in insatiable heat. But I was not to see her for some time.

Though I was devoting more of my efforts to Lionel, he began to show worrisome changes. He couldn't remember the day of the week before stressful lessons, especially those dealing with the anatomy of the brain and all its highly complicated tracts and connections. I was managing, barely. I found the heart to be the most exciting organ, especially the marvelously intricate functional anatomy—or was it because I was a hopeless romantic?

"Lionel, the seat of the soul resides in the heart, according to Aristotle," I said to him one night.

He laughed wearily and said, "That's not what the Bible says. God resides in all of man, in all of us, even we Negroes."

He had a small radio in his room, an ancient Zenith, and he tuned in to the Armed Forces station that played good American jazz. When Louis Armstrong sang, he sang along with him, *"I'll get by, as long as I have you."* And he did a little tap dance to the music, trying to rouse himself.

But he was so lonely and frustrated that tears came to his eyes. He was a shy and humble man who could have had many friends, but he had convinced himself that white folks truly didn't care for the likes of him. He wasn't wrong. I could see the pain in his eyes when one of the students would casually ask him to turn his hand over so he could see if it was white on the surface of the palm, as in monkeys and apes. The students knew of the vicious attacks against the blacks in the South and knew all about the lynchings. Their efforts to be kind were cruelly condescending. They regarded blacks as poor, child-like victims.

One night, at the end of November, Lionel invited me to dine with him in one of the marvelous local restaurants.

"You know, it's Thanksgiving in the States. We will have our own Thanksgiving here."

The other American students kept much to themselves and made their own plans. We found a small bistro on the Rue de Bourg, and for five dollars we could ill afford we had a delicious six-course meal. We ordered coq au vin, the closest thing to turkey we could find on the menu, and a cheap Algerian wine. By the end of the dinner, we had both grown mellow and melancholy.

"You really miss your young lady," he said. "I see the sadness in your eyes. Man, you are young and good-looking. You will find dozens of others."

"Lionel, I know, but one needs time and some money."

I felt offended, hurt, when this beautiful young woman just disappeared out of my life. Embarrassment or maybe simply shyness prevented me from making inquiries about her. My ego was shattered. I concluded that I just wasn't good enough for her.

In the weeks that followed, I could study little and was still waiting for that gentle knock on my door that would relieve the weight of depression from me.

By the beginning of December I decided I needed to get out and decided to try a student restaurant. It was cold and raining, and I took the long walk to the medieval building through the dark, narrow streets of Toulouse. A pungent odor surrounded me from the sewage that flowed in the gutters.

The restaurant was crowded with French and Algerian students, all waiting in line with metal trays. I picked up a tray, along with a glass and some worn silverware. Military style, servers filled each section of the plate with French fries, sausages, and withered tomatoes, and poured Algerian table wine into our glasses. The cashiers required a student identity card, which I had never bothered to get from the bursar's office. Standing directly in back of me was a tall, scrawny black woman holding her tray, stacked with double portions of vegetables, meat, and two glasses of wine.

"Oh, he is American. Let him go by. I will explain everything to him," she said in French.

"*Merci*," I said to her, grateful for her concern and kindness.

"Don't waste your time in French. I'm an American. Follow me and I will teach you the ropes."

There were miles of long wooden tables in this school cafeteria, with the haggard and exhausted students eating from their metal plates. The smells of food permeated the air, mixed with smoke—such dense smoke—and wine and unwashed bodies and clothes. There wasn't another American in sight, except for my new friend, Clarice.

She found her own spot and thrust her thin body on the bench between two other students.

"So you came to join the Foreign Legion in Toulouse? You look like a bright kid. Why aren't you at Yale or some other spiffy joint?"

I didn't answer her.

"How long have you been here?" I asked.

"Five years," she said, "and I will stay until I pass my exams. This is a good place to learn French," she said, "but you need a girlfriend to really learn the language. Do you have any money?"

"No."

"Too bad. That will make it very hard. With money you

get slides, a good skeleton, good English texts, and even tutors. And, of course, you need money to take a woman for coffee."

"Do you have money?" I asked her.

"*C'est drole,* that is funny. Would I be eating in this prison cafeteria? I manage."

Her hair was unkempt, she looked shabby, but she burst with life and enthusiasm. Most of the students who passed us greeted her. I must have met a dozen of these in only a few minutes.

"Come home with me. I have a roommate you may like. She speaks no English, but you aren't a bad-looking guy."

We finished eating and left the cafeteria. We walked with long quick strides through the windy streets for almost an hour. Finally we reached a row of small houses.

"We live on the ground floor: two bedrooms, a kitchen, a small living room."

"Danielle!" she yelled. "We have a visitor."

Strewn on the floor and on the kitchen table were books and papers.

"I will make some coffee," Clarice said. "Push them aside and find a spot. I usually sit on the floor."

She continued speaking while she made the coffee, but I was unable to hear a word.

Danielle came into the room wearing a housecoat. The light in the room was dim, but I could see she had dark hair and was buxom, with large round eyes. She was not a particularly attractive woman, and she appeared considerably older than I.

"There you are, Danielle. Were you sleeping? This is our new friend, an American medical student. He has to learn French because he will never pass."

"*Enchanté,*" she said.

We all sat on the floor drinking coffee, while Clarice chatted on, and then she suddenly rose and said, "I have to study and leave you two alone. When you leave, you can borrow my bones. I have a very good skull, femur, radius, pelvis, and hand. The rest you will have to scrounge around for. You have to learn each crease on the bones and holes in the skull and what goes through them. If you pass anatomy, you are on your way. Most of the students flunk anatomy and bio-chemistry the first time around."

Danielle was able to follow some of my English, and we limped along. It grew late. Classes began at eight in the morning, and I wondered how I would get back.

There were no buses. Clarice solved my dilemma when she rejoined us.

"It's too late to go back to your hotel," she said. She must have read my thoughts. "Stay here and we can leave together in the morning. You can sleep with Danielle. She won't mind."

Clarice explained to Danielle, who simply said, "*d'accord,* all right."

Danielle's room was neat and organized. There was a cross on the wall and a wonderful painting of the Virgin Mary on her dresser. No books or magazines cluttered up her room. The night was chilly, and I was glad to be under the large down feather duvet. Soon she was beside me, her robe neatly folded over the chair.

It was good not to be alone. But all night I thought of Monique, even as we made love.

In Toulouse, the week or so before Christmas, there were few signs that the holiday was fast approaching. Here and there decorations bedecked the stores; occasionally, a Christmas tree was visible. Christmas in France was a serious, somber religious holiday. After midnight, after church, all the restau-rants and homes had a huge dinner, called Le Réunion. The Americans almost always took this time to go skiing or traveling, so the hotel was almost empty.

Lionel cooked a small goose and sweet potatoes on his stove, and we listened to the Armed Forces network program that played Christmas carols all night. We drank champagne and wine and sang along. It was hardly Christmas in Vermont, but it was Christmas.

After midnight, I staggered back to my room and fell asleep on my bed. I didn't hear the knock on the door, but I felt a gentle kiss on my cheek. Monique stood above me, perfumed, lovely in a red dress. Only the light filtering in from the hall entered the small room.

"Merry Christmas, *chéri*," she said, and handed me a Christmas card and a large chocolate heart. At first I was convinced I was dreaming but then I pulled her toward me.

In the morning, without makeup, she looked even more beautiful than the night before.

"Where have you been all these months? I waited and waited, disturbed and even annoyed. If only you had written or called me."

"Well, you know. It was better this way. My father was ill, and I had to stay in the country with my parents. Let's be happy," she said, "and we must begin Christmas Day the French way."

She returned a few minutes later with a bottle of champagne, two glasses, coffee, two croissants, and a small radio.

"We better stay home today. It is snowing too much."

In our rooms night and day were one. Monique brought two blue candles, a miniature Christmas tree, and a plastic reindeer in a glass. She owned a small turntable and a collection of Edith Piaf, Charles Trenet, Yves Montand, and Frank Sinatra. She transformed the small depressing room into a magic wonderland.

We laughed and made love and slept, and ate delicious French cheeses, and drank wine, and smoked Phillip Morris cigarettes.

When I felt hungry she made an omelet of herbs. We ate chocolate and bread in bed. Sometimes my eyes wandered to the section on the ceiling with my blackboard of biochemistry formulas. I strained to read them in the candlelight. Monique prevented me from returning to reality by placing her small delicate hands over my eyes.

"*Allons, petit chou,* there is time enough for your chemistry on the ceiling. There is enough here. *Fait le practique en moi,* practice on me."

We whispered like lovers, told of everything in our hearts while listening, enraptured, to Edith Piaf singing "Mon Amour."

"From now on we speak only in French," she said, "and if you don't understand, *tant pis,* too bad, your loss. You must learn French very well or you won't pass your exams."

An entire day and another night went by, and in the morning she left the room with all her lovely possessions.

I must confess that I had completely forgotten about Lionel, who must have surmised why I hadn't surfaced for nearly two days. I knocked on his door and was surprised not to see him at his desk. He kept his room immaculate. He didn't want "the white folks to think we Negroes are dirty."

All our rooms were malodorous, reeking, but not his. He used a pine spray. His bed was made, the towels neatly folded, and there was nothing in the room except for his cooking utensils and some cans of food, neatly stacked, a bottle of wine, and a carton of Phillip Morris. His clothing was gone, and there was a note on the desk and a large envelope addressed to me.

Dear Lover Boy:

I did not want to disturb you, but I have to leave. I am too lonely and it is no use. I can't ever learn all of this stuff. I tried, as you well know. I don't belong in medical school and will make out fine at home. You will be a great doctor someday, and I want to thank you for being so kind to an old man. Please take my oil cooker and food and radio. The envelope is for you. When you get your M.D. and make good money, you can repay me. What use are French francs to me anyway? Take care of yourself. Peace and love.

Inside the envelope were thirty thousand francs—about five hundred dollars! Enough money for me to finish off the year in luxury and to buy my own skeleton to study.

My throat was dry, my eyes moist. Dear kind Lionel, my irreplaceable friend. I would miss him always.

Monique had disappeared again for two days, and when she returned, late at night, she brought a little present, a "good luck pen."

"I didn't come to see you because you must study. It is very difficult to pass the exams here in France, you know, and I want to stay here with you, but if you do not succeed, I will be to blame."

"And if you don't come here, I will also fail because I cannot concentrate enough to study," I said. "So it is better you are here, and I will study like a mad fool, drawing energy from you." A smile and a pause. "Where do you disappear to? You are so mysterious."

"*Mon chéri,* mystery and longing are the secrets of lasting love, so we say in French."

"Where do you go?" I asked her again.

"Oh, you know, I have parents I must stay with in the country, outside of Toulouse. We live in a vineyard, and my father makes wine. Someday, we will perhaps go together."

On weekends, Monique became more generous with her time. Knowing we would soon see each other was the motivation I needed to work twice as efficiently during the week.

We met often in the center of town, at the Place Capitale, in the Cafés des Artistés, where, apparently, Toulouse Lautrec had once come to do some paintings.

"It is better that those nosy people in the hotel don't see us together," she said. "*Je suis très propre*, I am very moral, you know. In France, we keep our private lives very discreet."

It became apparent that Monique was educated, *au courant*, as the French say. She always looked as if she had just walked out of a stylish dress shop. Scarves of colorful silk were as much a part of her as her beautiful brown hair. She was wearing a leather coat, a blue and brown scarf draped casually around her neck as I approached the café one day. She was sitting demurely by a small round table near the window. The late afternoon light made her beautiful hair shimmer. She was sipping a cup of coffee, and just for a moment I wanted to look at her from a distance, objectively. Her small lips were on the porcelain rim of the cup; one of her adorable fingers with the red polish rested on her chin; her legs were tightly crossed, her ankles touching. She must have just arrived because her cheeks were fresh and red as apples from the cold December air.

When I approached her, her face lit up, and she said, "*Tiens, tiens, mon petit chou.* Did you work well?"

"Very well. So well I have the day free."

"And the night?"

"Of course, the night." She gave me a tiny kiss on the cheek, and her eyes glowed with such love and passion that I wanted to smother her with kisses right then and there.

Love makes you feel confident, unafraid. It gives you the strength and security to make fun of everything, and makes you want to laugh at that which once seemed terribly serious. Loving Monique gave me a sense of freedom I had never known. I could breathe again, drawing in huge and delicious gulps of clean air.

Now we were together most of the time. While I struggled nightly with the endless difficult studies, Monique stayed in my room. Languidly dozing on the bed or reading a book of poetry, she would catch my eye and wave to me as if from a distant field. Sometimes, she stole behind me and touched my head with her lips while her arms encircled my drooping shoulders. Slowly, I would turn my head and her face would be near mine. I followed the curve of her thin eyebrows with my fingers and touched her small, curved nose and her lips.

"Not yet, *mon dieu.* Go back to your histology. There are only a few months before the exams."

Like most of the other students, I had stopped attending classes because there was just not enough time to do everything. My day still began at five, now with Monique sleeping soundly while I brewed some Nescafé. Fatigue was one feeling I never felt now. So inspired, so driven was I, that even the grueling hours of study became enjoyable. Carnal pleasures and scholarly endeavors coexisted side by side, each prompting and enhancing the other.

We took the train to visit the ruins in Arles, the old museums and buildings in Montpelier, and one weekend we took the train to the Riviera.

Nice in the month of March was cold and windy. This great playground of the world now belonged to the people who made their home by the sea. The empty cafés looked like ghosts, and the hotels, even the famous Negresco, were stark and awesome–a grand lady asleep, without makeup, but still elegant and beautiful. The stony beach which soon would be covered with beautiful people was now washed by the sea. The salt air cleared my brain. In just a few hours I was reborn, eager to return to the job. Such wisdom in such a young woman to know exactly when I needed a rest.

As the days to the exams grew nearer, I became more

nervous, even neurotic. In the middle of our lovemaking, I would jump up from the bed to check on something I thought I had forgotten.

"*Mon dieu*, of all the men in the world, I have to fall in love with a medical student," she said. Nothing that Monique said or did could erase the accelerating madness in my brain, filled to overflowing with images of dancing arteries and nerve connections and complex and intricate formulas. My texts and I merged into one—a necessary but loveless marriage.

I saw Monique only once or twice a week as spring arrived. The air was fresh and gentle, the cafés alive again, majestically lining the streets filled with young lovers. Late at night, when Monique was not with me, I would take a break from my studies and walk through the old narrow streets of centuries-old houses. I would recite out loud whatever I had memorized that day. Onlookers must have taken me for a madman. Prostitutes of all sizes and shapes, young and old, stood along these dark, streets calling, "*Viens, chéri*, a little love in the night." It was part of the charm of Toulouse.

Some of the faces looked familiar to me because they were required by law to check in the clinic each week to be tested for venereal diseases. The medical students were assigned to their care, which was part of our clinical training. Their *cartes d'identités* had to be signed, stating they were free of disease. Otherwise they would be arrested by the police.

The final exams were like a lottery. Two subjects would be picked from a hat, and these would become the written portion. A passing grade entitled the student to take the oral examinations.

On the morning of the lottery, the students gathered in the medieval courtyard of the medical school. It was a lovely morning, and there was a carnival atmosphere. The younger students, those who had not flunked the examinations the first time around, were kicking a soccer ball. Others were smoking furiously, pacing back and forth. Monique and I stood in the shadows of the old pillars of the courtyard. She looked elegant and beautiful, her arm around me, my heart racing. It was impossible to know all the subjects in detail, especially anatomy. Each student hoped that the two subjects picked would be their strongest—for me, anatomy and biochemistry.

One of the proctors from the anatomy laboratory stood in the center of the circle of students, holding the traditional worn top hat containing white slips of paper, upon which, written in gold, were the names of each subject.

Monique pushed closer to my side, waiting for the chosen student to put a hand into the hat.

"It is histology and legal medicine!" he finally shouted. Some of the students groaned with pain while others cheered. I was absolutely crestfallen. Those were the subjects I had studied the least.

"Don't look so doomed," Monique said. "You have some weeks more before the exam and you can make a quick review, *n'est-cé pas?*"

The next three weeks were like a nightmare. I saw little of Monique.

"We must not drain any energy from you," she said. "I have a little present for you to make your brain better." She gave me a handful of vials with a green solution inside. It looked like something to put into a bath to make bubbles.

"It is glutamic acid. All the students use it. It makes you calm and helps you to memorize better." In Europe at that time you could get all kinds of drugs over the counter, and many samples were sent to medical students. Some of the students at the hotel relied on Maxidol, a drug that allowed them to stay awake and study all night.

I knew it was an amino acid, but I could not find it in the text. When Monique left, I threw the vials in the wastebasket.

The Hotel Henri became one large study hall. None of us slept much. We crammed desperately, trying to digest everything in our voluminous textbook. We formed small study groups and reviewed questions handed down by students who had gone before us. We had to know every crease on the bones of the body and skull, every formula, all the French laws pertaining to legal medical aspects of murder and genocide, euthanasia, and drug abuse.

During those grueling nights and days, Monique weaved in and out of the room, staying just long enough to be embraced. Most of the time I hardly noticed her, but her perfume filled the room; or she left some bread and cheese, or a paté or sausages or chocolates. My underclothes and socks were cleaned and folded neatly on the bed, and she left little notes: "*Mon petit chou,* work hard, I miss you."

By the middle of May, it was over. My brain felt sharp during the exams, but I dared not hope I passed. Euphoria mixed with silent prayers and sleepless nights while I waited for the results to be posted on the bulletin board of the medical school.

If I flunked, I half convinced myself that it mattered little as long as Monique was with me. This rationalization offered some relief from the strain. When word spread at the café at Place Capitale that the names of the successful candidates had been posted, we rushed like lunatics to the bulletin board, Monique holding and squeezing my icy hand. Some students came back cheering, others bemoaning their fate—another year of torture.

Monique insisted that she check the bulletin board for me.

"I will bring you good luck, my dearest."

I watched her trim body stretching to see the names, and

she returned a few minutes later, silently, with not a trace of expression on her face.

"*Eh bien, mon docteur,* you passed!" she squealed and flung her arms around me and wouldn't stop kissing my teary eyes. We jumped and danced, squeezed until our ribs hurt.

Even though the many years ahead would be as trying as this one, I had passed the essential test of the first year. If I knew then what still lay ahead of me, I doubt that I would have continued. The first blow fell soon after, when I received a letter from the Board of Examiners in New York stating that it would no longer accept a degree from the Toulouse medical school. I would have to transfer to a medical school in Switzerland. This meant I would have to return to New York to work as a waiter in a summer resort. But none of that truly perturbed or disheartened me—except that I would have to leave Monique.

Everyone should be in love at least once in the spring. Old Toulouse became a garden of love. Miles of open-air cafés packed with young and old, sitting, talking, eating, thinking, in the young sun of the new day. Women in large aprons scrubbed the sidewalks in front of their homes. The outside markets, a kaleidoscope of colorful tulips and daffodils, intermingled with the displays of hundreds of cheeses, sausages, breads, meats, and fish. Everywhere were the smells and whispers of spring. It was intoxicating.

Monique and I were like hundreds of others, holding hands, bending our heads together, always kissing, sharing those wonderful sweet secrets and glances only lovers know.

My French was fluent now, thanks to Monique, and we rarely spoke in English. French was meant for making love.

"I want to know everything about you," I told her, "what you looked like when you were a child, your family, all your secret thoughts and fantasies; yes, even about all your lovers."

"*Mon dieu*, this is too much. A French woman never speaks of her old lovers. You want to possess me. You let me keep a little of myself, young doctor-to-be."

We were sitting on the concrete parapet facing the river, the Haute Garronée, that snakes through the Burgundy country and down to the region of France called the Midi. Men and women were there by the hundreds, fishing poles in hand.

"I am jealous of your dreams," I told her. "Each smile you give to someone else is a loss for me."

"*Arrête, mon petit fou*—stop, my little fool. That you have little experience with women is obvious. Of course we love each other today, it is spring. But tomorrow, when the bloom is off the rose, who knows? When you return from New York, you may come back married."

"Never. I don't want anyone else. You'll see. Wait for me."

I wrote to Monique every night from New York. She was with me every minute in spirit. She answered in her delicate handwriting. I tried to contact Lionel as well, but he was no longer at the address he had given me and all my letters were returned.

October finally arrived. I had survived the misery of the summer, knowing I would soon return to the country I had learned to love and to Monique. The smells and sounds and colors of Toulouse were with me each moment of the day. At least once a week a letter had arrived from Monique, but in the two weeks before I left for France, none arrived. Not hearing from her was agony.

In October, the sea becomes rough and exciting. I paced the decks of the Ile de France on its transatlantic crossing like a caged animal as the winds howled. Soon I would be seeing Monique, and neither a storm nor any power on earth was going to stop me.

Back in Toulouse, the concierge greeted me affectionately at the desk. Nothing had changed over the last few months. My eyes rested on the narrow circular stairs that led to the second floor, where once I lived in my room of paradise.

"Does Monique have the same room?" I asked.

"No, she is no longer here, Monsieur."

A sledgehammer hit my head.

"Where did she go?" I asked in panic. "Did she not leave a message? She knew when I was to arrive. I wrote her a dozen times."

"She was picked up by the police," he said quietly.

"The police? Monique? Are you sure? Why? What happened?"

"Eh bien, she did not go for a checkup and failed to register."

"Checkup? What are you saying?"

"In France, all the *pittaines* have to register, and a doctor examines them once a month."

"*Pittaine?*" Monique a prostitute? "Are you mad?"

"Everyone knew it," the concierge's wife said. "We were sure you did, too. We had warned her not to bother you, and we threatened to make her leave the hotel."

I felt drained of life.

"Please sit, Monsieur. We really did not know you were not informed. She never told you, or asked you for money?"

"Of course not. She brought me presents. I never gave her anything. She said she visited her parents' vineyards, not far from here, when she was away."

I grabbed the desk for support.

"I have to find her. I must see her. It is surely a mistake."

But it was not a mistake. The police had her registered as a whore, a call girl. After her mandatory medical checkup for venereal disease, she paid a small fine, was released, and had not been seen again. Sometimes I wondered what she found so wonderful about a poor medical student when she was so beautiful and alluring. She made love magnificently—an artist at her craft.

I turned away from the desk because I felt sick, my stomach knotted. I was dead inside. When I boarded the train several hours later for Switzerland, I thought, for an instant, that I saw Monique in her leather coat, a colorful scarf flying in the breeze, walking arm in arm with a man with gray hair.

COKE *on a* HOT DAY

1963

REVEREND COLLINS WAS AT THE FUNERAL, ALONG WITH family, friends, and patients of Dr. Allan Tisherman. The chapel ceremony took 20 minutes, and then the family and closest friends headed for the cemetery outside the city, following the gleaming hearse. The service was brief.

The day was oppressively hot, and I was on the way to my car when Reverend Collins touched my elbow. "Can you spare a few moments from your busy schedule, Doctor? Dr. Tisherman was our family physician for many years. Would you be willing to take my family on?"

"Certainly. I would be honored."

Reverend Collins was the Methodist leader in the community, an important and influential man. Having him as a patient would be a windfall. I knew that many more would follow.

"Stop by this evening," he said, "and I'll give you the files Dr. Tisherman left."

I had met Dr. Tisherman several years earlier when I was a resident and he was an attending physician. Tall and lean, he was an impressive figure in his white coat. He rarely discussed medicine, but chatted easily about everything from books to sailing and the business end of medical practice.

I met his wife and his children for the first time at the funeral parlor. She politely thanked me for coming and asked if I wouldn't mind covering his practice until things got sorted out. I was struck by how businesslike she was, how reserved and even serene.

When I arrived that evening, Reverend Collins was sitting in his living room in his shirt sleeves, wearing a bow tie. A pair of reading glasses sat low on his nose. He rose from the chair at his desk, greeting me warmly.

"You're going to be a very busy doctor," he told me. "Dr. Tisherman's patients have been calling all afternoon to find a new doctor."

The Reverend continued talking as he reached into one of the desk drawers and brought forth a stack of folders.

"These are his records. Dr. Tisherman was quite a compulsive man. Everything just right and in perfect order. Nothing out of place."

"How pitiful that he died at the height of his career," I said.

He looked up, his eyes unmoved. "It would have been a tragedy had he lived," the Reverend said softly. When I frowned, he said, "Don't look so shocked, young man. Did you know Dr. Tisherman?"

"Only superficially."

"I think I must tell you, then, something about him in complete confidentiality, of course, since you will be seeing most of his patients. They are, by and large, good people, rich and solid citizens, the backbone of this congregation." He settled himself into a frayed armchair, his glasses even lower on his nose.

"Well, Al Tisherman came to our town eighteen years ago, with his wife. He had just finished his training in New York, and decided not to go back to his hometown, Philadelphia. He wasted no time at all finding out exactly what clubs to join, where to be seen, and he soon sat on the Board of Education and attended all the Town Hall meetings. He was quite brazen. It was part of his charm. We don't drink alcohol in our house, so the first time he came here my wife served milk. He asked for a beer.

"'Why did you pick a small town? You're obviously a city slicker. New York or Philadelphia would be your speed, it seems to me,'" I told him.

"'I wanted to raise children amidst oaks and hemlocks and gardens, and in peace and safety, to get to know my neighbors, to feel that I'm part of the community.'

"Well, I asked him if he would like to take care of our family, and we became his first patients. It didn't take long for him to really settle in. I mentioned his charm, and he had quite a sense of humor, especially appreciated by the old folks. He had a special knack with them, like no other doctor I'd ever seen.

"Would it be of any interest to tell you that I've seen a great deal of the world from my missionary work in East China? I was a prisoner of the Japanese, spent four years in Vietnam before the French came, and then three years in the jungle of San Paula. I did all these things as a young man, until, you understand, we decided to have a family. So we settled down here in this little city. I know a little bit of the world, Doctor, and her people, but in all the world I never met anyone quite like Dr. Tisherman."

At that moment the phone rang. It was for me. The call came from the emergency room and made me feel both disappointed and relieved. I was curious, but growing a bit weary of the Reverend's speech.

"Well, another time," he said. "Soon?"

"Of course."

The town was heavy with humidity as early evening arrived. The emergency room held an air of agitation, and tempers were sharp, quick. There was no end to the people who arrived suffering knife wounds, automobile traumas, bad drug trips—as if all humanity were on a massive suicide mission.

"Oh, you aren't Dr. Tisherman," a tiny elderly woman said in a tone heavy with disappointment. "He knows me so well."

"I'm attending to his patients for now," I said gently.

"When will he be back? I have to see him. Can't you get in touch with him and just tell him that Mrs. Cody needs him? Not that you aren't a good doctor, young man. You have a nice, kind face. It's just that I've got one of those dizzy spells again. It scares me so, living alone. Don't you see? I need Dr. Tisherman."

She looked so fragile and delicate, so birdlike, her gray hair tied in a small bun, lying there alone and clearly frightened. She soon began to cry, in muffled sobs.

"Everything is all right," I told her. "You will be fine." But no matter what I said, it had no impact on her. She wanted her own doctor. I could only hope to inspire such loyalty one day in my patients. She left before I had a chance to explain what had happened.

And it didn't end there. The next day saw a steady procession of patients of Dr. Tisherman's. Each one seemed more devoted to him as the dreary afternoon wore on. Some had learned of his sudden demise and were so shattered by his death that they couldn't have grieved more had he been a member of their immediate family.

Several days later I managed to get to Dr. Tisherman's office. It was sparsely decorated and immaculately neat. Each of the patient charts that I inspected was neat, concise, and precisely followed the format taught in medical school. What struck me about the patients was that none seemed really ill. Other than minor complaints, all of them suffered only from fatigue, some loss of memory, depression, or loneliness. After borrowing some of the charts, I asked if I could also borrow some medications from the doctor's cabinet, some injectables I thought I might need.

"I don't see why not," the receptionist said. "He's certainly not going to need them any longer."

Some of the shelves were stacked with small brown bottles, dozens and dozens of them. They were unlabeled, but each contained a white snowy powder. I was too embarrassed to ask what it was, not wanting to display my ignorance or to intrude.

No one was coming to my own office yet, so I settled into his. The first patient the next day was a tense elderly man with an impressive, almost noble face. He had arrived for his monthly checkup.

"What has Dr. Tisherman been treating you for?" I asked.

"Don't you see it in the chart?" he answered belligerently.

"Not really. It indicates that you are doing fine, and that there are no problems."

"Of course I have problems." He cited a laundry list of symptoms which suggested disorders from the tip of his head to the bottom of his toes—a table of contents from a medical text.

"And what does Dr. Tisherman give you for all these complaints?"

"Well, he has his own treatment. He gives me some medications."

"Does he give the medication in his office?"

"Oh, yes indeed! He inserts the medications into my nose, into each nostril, and that keeps me comfortable for a little while. So, if you don't mind, Doctor, I'd like to have my usual treatment, which is long overdue anyway, I can tell you that much," he said anxiously.

"I don't know what Dr. Tisherman has given you. It doesn't appear on the chart."

"Well, then, you must certainly know. You're a doctor, too. What does one prescribe for these symptoms?"

"Well, see for yourself. You can look at your own chart. What does one prescribe?"

The man was eighty-three, had his own teeth, and, much to my surprise, didn't wear glasses. He began to read the chart.

"This isn't correct. I'm ninety-three," he said matter of factly. "Dr. Tisherman has given me treatment whenever I need it. He also gives me injections."

I was at a complete loss. Then I remembered the rows of little bottles with the white powder in them, and the doctor's magical treatment became suddenly all too clear.

The old man left, disappointed and angry, and told the receptionist he would find another doctor because I gave him no treatment.

That evening I returned to see Reverend Collins.

"I thought you'd be back tonight," he said. "Oh, yes, Dr. Tisherman left his patients quite happy, which I gather you've discovered by now. I found out about it one day a few months ago. I wasn't feeling myself, and I thought I was having a stroke. I went to see my good doctor friend, and he suggested I take a good sniff of his medicine. It was, he said, a medicine that was centuries old, an ancient Indian remedy."

"How could he have been dispensing cocaine all those years? Didn't the drug enforcement agencies get after him?"

"Well, after he became really successful, the money was rolling in and his practice grew enormously. I think almost everyone in the city must have switched to Dr. Tisherman. He relocated to a new big house, joined the country club, bought a vacation home in Florida and a ski home in Vermont. The children went to private school, his wife had a new car almost every year, and everything seemed swimmingly well. Then the good doctor started to get bored.

"He began to miss his dinners, and then he'd come home a bit later each night. You guessed it. He had a lady friend, a charming younger woman—likable, tall, efficient. The patients liked her, and so did the doctor. She was the model secretary, and obviously more. The good doctor went to more and more medical meetings. He planned everything very carefully. She became a friend of the family. His wife enjoyed her company, and she did her best to help his wife out with her correspondence or whatever else was needed. When they took trips to Europe, they brought her along so she could act as a babysitter for the children."

"How do you know all these things?" I asked.

"Tisherman told me everything, and his lady friend came to talk to me, too. Much of my time is spent listening to other people's indiscretions.

"The young secretary had other boyfriends, younger men than the doctor—truck drivers, bricklayers, roofers— all unknown to Dr. Tisherman, of course. She was the one who got him started. First, she introduced him to marijuana, which he was very reluctant to take, but he did it for her, and, after a while, the marijuana began to please him. Next, they started on cocaine, and she suggested that he could write prescriptions for it to ease his patients' pain. They knew what they were taking and kept coming back for more. Dr. Tisherman began working with more energy, and he took on sports that only a young man would hazard. He bought a motorcycle, and his blond friend kept urging him on, complimenting him on how handsome he was, how youthful and strong.

"One day I decided I'd better take a look into what was

going on. After all, I was his friend, and now he was a dashing figure racing around town on a motorcycle. He came to see me and was sitting right where you are now, his eyes glowing like diamonds. His speech was rapid, colorful, nonstop, as if someone had wound him up. I told him, 'You're changing so fast, I can't keep up with you. Do you have any problems you'd like to talk over?'

"'Me, problems? By God, no! Things have never been better. Why do you ask? Did one of my patients complain about me?'

"'No, nothing like that, except…Well, you know, the motorcycle, the young lady…'

"'The young lady is my secretary and friend, and my wife cares for her as much as I do. She's like family now. She shops with my wife, she baby-sits for us, and she's a loyal friend and a great secretary, nothing else. Understood?'

"'Nothing else?'

"He stood up straight, indignant, his eyes flaring in anger.

"'Nothing else! I love my wife and my children. You have no right to put me on the spot like this.'

"He was so angry that he stormed out of the house, and I watched him through the window begin running to his own house, leaving his motorcycle behind.

"That night I went to the high school gym, and there he was, in shorts, playing ball and running with the teenagers, sweating and laughing, carrying on with the boys. Toward the last half of the game, running and screaming for someone to pass the ball, he suddenly fell and lay very still. When I ran over to him he was clutching his chest and breathing heavily. They brought him to the hospital. A heart attack.

"He survived, and two months later he was back at work, doing twice as much as before, if that was possible. He wouldn't hear about taking on a partner. This was all about five years ago. He was thirty-five, and another change took place in him overnight. He shed his mod clothing, groomed his hair carefully, dressed immaculately in dark shades, wore only shoes imported from England. He dressed like an elegant physician of a hundred years ago, in a black jacket and striped pants. Twice a year he took his wife to Harrods in London and arranged to have a tailor send him his ties and shoes, even his underwear and handkerchiefs.

"He made lots of money and there was no end to his spending. Dinner was served by a butler on linen tablecloths, fine china, and Waterford crystal. He hired a French cook to prepare gourmet dishes. At first his family found it all a treat, but the children soon couldn't stand the routine of dressing for dinner each night, and Dr. Tisherman began to eat alone with his wife. They kept moving into bigger houses until he found a mansion with a winding staircase, surrounded by old oaks and majestic hedges, overlooking Long Island Sound. He developed a carriage practice—a gentleman practitioner—and kept increasing his fees. His poorer patients, of course, had to find other physicians. As his clientele became even wealthier, his eccentricities increased.

"Each morning it became a ritual before he left the house to spend one hour grooming his face and body with all sorts of creams and pomades, inspecting each newfound crease, unhappily following the lines on his face as he would the markings of a road map. Fresh flowers had to be on his desk, as well as in his lapel. His obsession with aging and seeing the older patients arrive with their chronic complaints caused him great despair. He did research on aging and treatments used in Europe to keep people looking young: placental injections, concoctions of gonads, vitamins and cocaine. After reading Freud's description of cocaine, he decided that he would use it in his own practice when his lady friend brought it up. It was immediately and impressively effective, and he used it more and more. He told me about it, but I couldn't dissuade him. He was driven, possessed.

"He reasoned, 'Why should cocaine be restricted to certain groups of people—musicians, artists, actors? Why should it not be used more freely, openly, by people who might really benefit from it in a basic psychological sense?'

"He rationalized his own addiction.

"'Freud,' he said, 'had written much of his great theory of psychoanalysis while on cocaine. Great surgeons did their most productive work on cocaine.'

"He tried his first treatment on a patient by the name of Jake Abrams, a lonely miserable soul who was well into his eighties, a man who had lost his wife and son. Each day, Jake prayed for death to come. His health was reasonably good, but he did suffer from beginning senility as well as arthritis of the joints. Jake had plenty of money, so he went to all the clinics and saw the most renowned specialists throughout the country. Tons of pills and treatments were tried on him, none of which helped at all. Besides being depressed, he lost his appetite and he began to lose weight. It was against his religious beliefs to commit suicide, which he would otherwise have eagerly accomplished. Just to pull himself out of bed and dress took half the morning. It wasn't that he was terminally ill, but that he was so full of pain and despair that he wished only to die.

"Each week Jake came to see Dr. Tisherman, who gave him his special treatment. The old man began to change gradually. He smiled more, paid closer attention to his personal care. By the end of three weeks, he had become a dapper gentleman, impeccably groomed, carrying a silver cane. It mattered little to him what it cost. For the first time in years, he had the will to live. He refurnished his apartment and got himself a girlfriend, even went back to his lifelong hobby of painting.

"And so it went, more or less, with all the others. Their

lives became bearable. Hopeless old women now appeared lively and youthful and optimistic. Word spread like fire in a dry forest and Dr. Tisherman had to turn patients away. Those he accepted had to wait months to see him. He selected only the most desperate and hopeless. One look into his waiting room and it became evident why he was so successful. It was filled with happy faces—eager, alert, elderly patients delighted with life. He devised fantastic ideas of buying an island in the Caribbean and converting it into a complete Paradise for the aged, Eden reborn for the elderly.

"Then, one week ago, on a particularly hot summer day, three men arrived at his office and served him with a warrant for his arrest. The patients watched, startled and disheartened and disbelieving, as agents escorted him out. The federal authorities confiscated hundreds of vials of cocaine that he had in his office, though there were plenty more. He was arraigned and released on bail. His wife and children were staying at their summer home in East Hampton. Dr. Tisherman returned to his own house and changed into a pair of slacks and a wool shirt.

"One of his neighbors saw him take a shovel from the tool shed and march out to his garden and begin to dig a trench. He had taken an extra large dose of cocaine and began to dig furiously, for hours, until he dug a trench six feet long. He was perspiring freely, but not weakened for one moment. The cocaine gave him the extra strength he knew he would need.

"By sunset, he had accomplished what he had planned. Only now did he begin to stagger, to become increasingly weak. He was a good enough physician to recognize that his damaged heart would not be able to tolerate such strain and heat. He crawled into the ditch, and that's where they found him. The newspaper reported his death as a tragic heart attack that occurred while he was working in the garden.

"His wife and children were left with ample insurance and money, but, unfortunately, tragically, he left a practice full of addicted patients—that's what he left for you to take over, if you want it.

"I told you that he was better off dead. But, I wonder, was it really so wrong, what he did? He was, after all, rendering a medical service to a lost generation of elderly people, burdens to their families, unwanted and misplaced individuals. He gave them new hope and aspirations, reasons to live. He gave them peace and even cheer."

"Unfortunately, Reverend," I answered, "cocaine gives a false temporary euphoria, and it is only a matter of time before it destroys people, body and soul. There are no shortcuts in caring for the sick and lonely. Cocaine is not the answer. It seems to me that Dr. Tisherman was using his patients to justify his own addiction."

I walked away from Dr. Tisherman's office and never returned. But I often think about doctors, long ago and today, who abuse drugs themselves and make them available to patients. We are the gatekeepers of medicine, but I am ashamed that some of us abuse that privilege.

ELI'S CURE

1964

My new cardiology practice included many Italians from nearby towns and farms in Connecticut, referred by a grateful life insurance salesman named Joe. He was a retired test pilot who had grown up in a strict Catholic Italian family that ran a small grocery store in New Haven. With each office visit he brought me a bottle of wine, grapes, tomatoes, figs—whatever was in season. Joe's lovely wife, Gwen, even became my medical assistant.

After six months in practice, my waiting room was typically filled with patients. Everything was going better than I had expected. Then one morning Gwen interrupted a consultation to whisper that there was someone on the line from the Attorney General's Office in Washington. She sounded petrified and my pulse began to race. I tried to think fast. Should I call a lawyer? Were they going to investigate me because of my Italian patients? Robert Kennedy, the tough new Attorney General, had made a pledge to go after the Mafia.

Any federal or local agency scared me. Just seeing someone in uniform or with a badge on his jacket made my heart skip a beat. The fear of being arrested and put away was a residue from my youth in Danzig when the brown shirts, Hitler Youth, and SS persecuted my family. Often I was attacked by Hitler Youth gangs on my way to school. Much of my family would perish in the Holocaust. My parents, my brother, and I escaped in 1938 only because my father was an important coal merchant and was able to buy us passage on the Queen Mary.

Even after arriving in New York City, I still was attacked because I was Jewish. We still lived in fear that someone was going to take us away. Decades later, nothing could take away this feeling of vulnerability, even though I had become a respected physician.

So it was with a lump in my throat that I picked up the phone. The caller, who turned out to be respectful and polite, had been referred to me by the Yale Medical School. He needed an expert opinion on the cardiac condition of an individual in custody.

I was flabbergasted and speechless for a moment.

"Of course. I would be honored," I replied.

"What will be your fee?" the man asked.

I blurted out, "Fifty dollars." Was that too much?

"OK," the man answered.

I should have asked for more.

I was the first to arrive at my office the following Monday. The phone was already ringing.

"Hey, Doc, you're gonna examine one of my friends," a gruff voice stated. "The Feds are bringing him to see you."

"Who is this?"

"You let this guy go, understand? You will regret it if you don't, and your family will, too. Understand? You make your report he can't be incarcerated," the caller continued, accenting each syllable of "incarcerated."

I didn't know what to say, but it didn't matter. The caller had hung up.

I was filled more with anger than fright. While uniforms

and badges made me feel vulnerable, for some reason I was never intimidated by common criminals and thugs.

What hubris and audacity, I thought, for him to try to interfere in the sacred doctor-patient relationship.

Twenty minutes later two tall, thin men who looked like they'd been sent from FBI central casting walked in, pulling an older man with curly hair, a grayish complexion, and a head as large as a horse's. Despite being handcuffed and short of breath, he smiled at me and seemed friendlier than the stolid agents, who flashed their badges and handed me a leather briefcase filled with medical reports.

"You expect me to read all these?" I asked.

"That's up to you. You're the doctor," the taller of the agents answered.

I was about to mention the threatening phone call, but looking at the patient, who didn't seem like someone who would harm my family, I decided to hear his story first.

One of the agents stayed in the waiting room, but the taller one insisted on coming with us to my exam room and removed the patient's handcuffs. He left us alone only when I declared the sacredness of the doctor-patient relationship.

The patient, whom I will call Eli, spoke in a soft, intelligent voice. He was suffering from severe coronary artery disease and angina. The famous Texas doctor Denton Cooley had written that if Eli went to jail, he would die in a few months. Dr. Cooley's mentor, Dr. Debarked, agreed. But the federal government wanted this guy behind bars and they had come to me for a third opinion. They wouldn't tell me what crime or crimes he had committed, only that mine would be the final determination.

Eli gave a convincing history of chest pain with effort and severe shortness of breath. This was in an era before stress tests and cardiac cauterization.

But it was quite evident that Eli was prone to sudden

death and not by electric chair but by his own lifestyle. He was only in his early thirties, like me, but his heart was that of an old man.

The more I chatted with him, the more I began to like him. After I finished my examination, I told Eli that I agreed with Dr. Cooley that he did have severe heart disease and added, "But I disagree that you shouldn't be incarcerated."

Eli's smile vanished, his face turned red, and he looked as if he was ready to strike me.

"Now listen for a minute," I told him. "Your diet and lifestyle are already a death sentence. If you go free you will be dead in a few weeks or months with the crowd you hang around. But I happen to know that Dr. Cooley is doing a new experimental surgical procedure. If you go to jail and have chest pain, they will put you in the hospital and I think you will qualify for it."

Eli eyed me suspiciously, but he knew he was at death's door and ultimately agreed.

I wrote my report and made the Attorney General happy. Eli went to prison. Three months later I received a large wreath of carnations with the note: "Doc, thanks. I was operated on and am doing fine."

I also received a fifty-dollar check from the Attorney General's Office, which I never cashed. It hangs framed on the wall behind my desk.

And the name of the experimental procedure? Coronary artery bypass surgery.

GUYS and DOLLS
1964

O N JULY 12, 1964, I GRADUATED FROM THE YALE SCHOOL of Medicine and decided to open a practice in Internal Medicine. I rented a small suite in the Doctor's Building in New Haven, though the building's owner discouraged it: "Too many doctors in New Haven. Go to Darien or Bridgeport." He ran a carriage practice, which means his patients were mainly rich folks from the suburbs. That afternoon, in defiance to his advice, I signed a contract for the office and went searching for furniture.

As I had no assets after fifteen years of schooling, just huge debts, I applied for a loan and was refused. "But I am an M.D. and a Yale graduate," I pleaded with the loan officer.

"But that ain't no good, Doc. No assets, no loan."

A man who happened to overhear the conversation offered to co-sign for the loan. I'd never met him and would never see him again, but thanks to him I was able to furnish and decorate the office. I covered the walls with all of my degrees and my medical license, but I had no patients. Medical groups were just starting in those days. Most people practiced solo. There were no starting salaries as today from medical groups, but I did get six dollars an hour from the Yale Student Medical Clinic twice a week. My pregnant wife and I lived in a small apartment at the poverty level, eating our meals very cheaply in the hospital cafeteria.

The building where I worked also housed an insurance company, which gave me an idea. I asked if they needed anyone to perform their insurance physicals and said I'd charge ten dollars per examination. I was hired on the spot.

In the garage standing up behind an old Chevrolet, I examined a man by the name of Meurice. He was a tall, muscular man with a smart-looking face and the tough accent of a tough person. He was a graduate of Vanderbilt, but apparently was now the local mafioso, running the gambling scene and other vices, but not drugs.

The following morning, my office was crowded with seedy characters, some with flattened noses and broad shoulders. They looked like extras from Guys and Dolls. Meurice announced, "You pay the doc after he examines you." They did, and soon I had a distinguished non-carriage practice.

One of my new patients, a man allegedly named Bill, came staggering in looking as pale as a bride's dress. He was bleeding internally and I decided to admit him to the hospital. He refused to go by ambulance, but he did consent to have his colleagues drive him. When I arrived to see him that evening, he was settled in the hospital's best private room.

Outside his room sat two men who looked like goons from a late-night horror movie. They would not allow me to enter. Once I identified myself, they straightened up as if I was an army general and let me pass. Inside, the room looked like a flower shop. Huge red and blue reefs were scattered around the room, and an endless row of white gardenias lay across the floor. It gave the hospital room the appearance of an elaborate funeral parlor.

"Bill" was in bed, his face no longer pale. He had received several pints of blood and his eyes now moved about sharply, like a wild animal eyeing his enemy. As I came nearer to his bed, two of his hoodlums came close to me. "Hey, he's my doc—back off," he said in a garbled voice.

"Hey, Doc, when can I get out?" asked the same voice. I wanted to say, "I am not the warden, just the doctor." I explained to him that he was bleeding from a gastric ulcer and needed some time to heal. In those days, we only had antacids, not blood or surgery to cure an ulcer. "Just a few days, Bill, and you will be free to go," I told him. "You have to stop smoking, drinking, and no aspirin."

"What—are you kidding? I can't live like that. And no broads, I suppose," he stated. The male chorus by the door erupted in laughter.

"I never restricted your sexual activity," I told him.

"Sexual activity? Is that what you Ivy guys call it?" he asked, and they roared again.

It was a particularly hot, humid day in August, and those patients who could leave their beds went out to the fire escapes for relief. From a distance, they looked like birds resting on tree branches. There were fans in the rooms, but they were turned off, and the patients and doctors sweated profusely. The doctors were buttoned up to their necks in white. The chief residents wore short-sleeved white shirts and striped ties. (At that time, there were hardly any women interns or residents.) The nurses moved in stiff white uniforms and caps. There were no nurse practitioners, just male orderlies and nursing assistants. Doctors were still regarded with great respect and dignity. It was an honor to be a doctor during those golden days of medical practice, before government and insurance companies ruled the practice of medicine. It was a particular honor to have attending medical privileges at this hospital, as they were granted only to those people who had trained at Yale.

At home that evening, I received a frantic call from the hospital asking me to rush in to see Bill. In my old Buick, I sped through lights, swinging my stethoscope out the window as a sign to any squad cars what my business was. I rushed up to the 8th floor and into the private room expecting Bill to be in shock or even dead. "You just missed him," the resident stated.

"What happened?" I asked with a panicked but authoritative tone.

"Your patient, in his nightdress, with his entourage, climbed down the fire escape out to the street and into a large limousine. He did not bother to check out."

We never saw Bill again, but his girlfriend did pay the hospital charges.

In the
STROKE
WARD
CIRCA 1965

T HE PATIENT IS LYING ON HIS BACK IN THE STROKE WARD of the hospital, unable to move or speak. An intravenous drip runs into his right arm, and small round discs are attached to his chest, connected by wires to a monitor over his head. Nasal prongs are in his nose.

Every hour someone comes to care for him. A nurse takes his blood pressure and adjusts his pillow. He can tell day from night because in the morning the interns and residents come by. At night, a short medical student keeps touching the stethoscope to his chest as if listening for some faraway chant.

Today, after the doctors finished rounds, he was transferred onto a stretcher and taken to the X ray department for a CAT scan of his head. For almost one hour he has been waiting in the cold, futuristic corridor. Other people are on stretchers around him, lined up as if at a starting gate at the racetrack. People stare at his drooping eyelids and sagging jaw as he drools like an infant; his eyes are unable to close.

When it is his turn, he notices that the scanner makes a sound that reminds him of what he heard as a boy when he would run while pulling a stick across a picket fence.

Back in the stroke unit, everything is clean and shiny. The prongs are settled into his nose again, delivering oxygen to his half-dead brain. It's five o'clock in the afternoon, feeding time. A nurse attaches a large plastic bag containing a fluorescent fluid to the long silver pole next to his bed. It hangs like a colored lantern at a luau.

It is night again, and there is more noise than during the day. The lights are dim, and everything looks dreary. There is a small room by the stroke unit where the orderlies and nurses smoke cigarettes and drink coffee. The music they play at night comes from a large portable box radio—not the kind of music he likes to hear. They switch the station to something familiar, Wagner's "Ride of the Valkyries," the same music that blasted from a Nazi truck as it passed through the streets of his childhood village.

His mind begins to wander back in time. He is on a bench with his mother and father in a room at the Gestapo headquarters. There is no sound except the noise from the loudspeaker of the truck and the singing, "Deutschland über Alles." They take his mother and father away, and he begins to cry.

Now, as he lies here, he can't stop the tune from going through his head. His lips move as if to sing, but no sound emerges.

The next morning the doctors stroke his feet to see if he has any reflexes, and a speech therapist tries to get him to form words. All he can say is über.

In the afternoon he can't move his arms or his legs. His wife and children visit twice a day, and he can't bear to see their sad faces.

"I think you are enjoying this," the nurse says as she gives him a sponge bath.

"Ja," he says.

"Are you comfortable?"

"Ja, danke."

"He can only speak German," she whispers to an intern.

Lying in bed, staring at the ceiling, he sees two tiny creatures slowly climbing down the wall toward the bed. They look like maggots. They seem headed for his face, undisturbed by all the tubes and all the people in the room.

The creatures begin to crawl on his head, climbing over the electrodes placed there. Surely, he thinks, someone will see. The creatures walk through all the connections, now exploring the tube in his penis, now the tubes in his artery, now the tube in his vein. They seem to have settled on a destination, attracted to the hissing of the oxygen as it escapes the prongs in his nose. Slowly, slowly, they move along the plastic lifeline and climb inside, up the nostrils, along the frontal sinuses, through the small holes and up into the convoluted dead brain tissue.

Six weeks later the speech therapist is frustrated because he can only say a few words in German, and the physical therapist is trying out braces for his dead arms and legs. The plastic surgeon has kept him from getting ulcers on his backside by meticulously debriding dead tissue. A special floating bed keeps his body suspended during the day, swinging as if in a hammock. Electrodes stimulate his muscles, which twitch like the frog he remembers dissecting in biology class.

He's still paralyzed, and the invaders are still burring their way through his nasal system. Since all the nerves have been eaten away, he no longer feels any pain. He sees his reflection briefly when the barber cuts his hair and shaves him. The nose is getting bigger, more swollen. He is beginning to get some feeling back in his arms and legs.

His wife asks the nurse why his nose looks so big and discolored.

"It's from the nasal prongs," comes the nurse's explanation.

A couple of mornings later, the roof of his nose caves in like a mineshaft, releasing oxygen into the room.

An X ray of his nose reveals that the septum has been destroyed. The doctors are baffled, wondering whether he has been sniffing cocaine. An ear, nose, and throat specialist is called in. After examining the patient for an hour with a nasal speculum, he removes two live maggots. No one can guess how they might have gotten there, and the patient cannot tell them.

A LIFT
CIRCA 1974

IN THE MID-1970S I ATTENDED THE AMERICAN COLLEGE OF Cardiology's annual meeting in Miami. I spent five days in the dark watching slides and listening to the speakers reading from their notes.

At the end of the conference I waited at the end of a long line for a taxi to take me to the airport. After nearly one hour, I decided to walk away from the hotel to look for a cab down the street. I waited for a good half hour, carrying my suitcase and stopping to rest as I watched the cab drivers racing past me with their passengers. My plane back to JFK was due to depart in two hours, and if I missed it I would have to spend another night in Miami.

On the side of the road where I stopped to rest was a small bungalow, outside of which was a round plastic table where four elderly men, shirtless, in shorts, were playing cards. They looked up and stared at me and at my suitcase.

"If you are a salesman, we are not interested, so keep marching, buddy," one of them said.

"I am not a salesman, but I have a proposition for you," I told them.

"Here we go," the oldest-looking of the men said. "A free trip to the Bahamas or to Las Vegas. Go ahead, what is the deal, Buster? I heard them all."

"How would you like to make twenty-five dollars to drive me to the airport?" I yelled to them. "I can't get a cab and I want to make the 12:30 flight back to New York, and you gentlemen look like you could help me out."

"Make it thirty-five and you got a deal," the older one said.

Another of the card players said, "I'll come, too. He doesn't know how to get to the airport, and it's my car." The three of us got into a beaten-up old Buick Le Sabre. I sat in the back with my luggage. I was grateful that these two men were going to help me out. They argued back and forth on the directions, and for a while it seemed we might never start the journey.

Harry, the driver, asked if I'd been at the meeting, if I was a heart doctor and where I was from. I was reluctant to carry on a conversation with them, fearing it would distract them from their driving.

"I'm from New York," I told him.

"I could tell from your accent," he said. "I am from Brooklyn, I have been here for ten years, since my wife died. I used to work in the garment industry, down on Thirty-eighth Street. The good old days: you get a frank on a roll for a dime, the Dodgers were still in Brooklyn, and Pee Wee was the best shortstop in baseball."

"I work in New Haven, Connecticut, now," I told him. "And I was a Dodgers fan, too, until they left New York."

We continued this banter as Harry drove at twenty miles per hour, cars around us honking. Then he suddenly dropped his hands off the steering wheel. He grew pale. He managed to steer the car onto the side of the road and stop on the grass.

His friend yelled, "Harry, what's wrong with you?"

Harry did not answer, turned blue and fell back on his seat. I rushed out, pulled his door open, and dragged him out onto the grass, where I pumped him on the chest.

"You breathe into his mouth while I pump," I yelled to

his friend, who looked like he was also going to pass out.

I had just listened to a lecture on CPR and presumed he went into cardiac arrest. I restarted his heartbeat as soon as I pounded on his chest. His friend had no need to give mouth-to-mouth breathing. Harry continued to speak as if nothing had happened. His color changed back to his tan. Passing drivers saw what was happening, and in few minutes a fire truck and an ambulance arrived. I went in the ambulance with Harry. We sped off to the hospital, passing many of the slow-moving taxis packed with my fellow conference attendees. Harry had suffered a myocardial infarction and cardiac arrest.

"Lucky thing you took my offer," I told him.

"Lucky, my ass," he snapped back. "All that traffic gave me the heart attack. And you still owe me thirty-five dollars."

EDITH

CIRCA 1978

"IS THE DOCTOR THERE?" THE FAMILIAR VOICE SOUNDED tense, even desperate.

"I am the doctor, you know that."

"Are you sure? You don't sound like him."

"But I assure you, it is me."

"Is there anyone else on the line?"

"No, there is no one listening. Speak freely."

There was a momentary silence as the grim voice on the other end of the line drew an agonized breath, then exhaled slowly, sounding as if she were forcing air into a seashell. She spoke in a husky whisper.

"Doctor, I think I have AIDS."

I was stunned into silence. Until that moment my only contact with this devastating new disease involved a few ward patients on the teaching medical service.

"What makes you think it is AIDS?" I finally asked.

"Did you read last night's local newspaper? There was a front-page article by a famous scientist at your hospital, listing all the symptoms. I have them all. Every damned one!"

Edith had been my patient for twenty years. Usually, patients I've known for so long become like members of my family, and I share with them all their successes and tragedies, even as they share mine. But I knew very little about Edith.

Her voice abruptly changed from a troubled whisper to her usual imperious tone. "I want you to run the AIDS test on me. But you people have no cure, and I am not going to be a guinea pig for some pharmaceutical house experimenting with a drug that won't work anyway. I've read all about that nasty business, Doctor. The medical school gets grant money from the drug company to try out some new concoction, which helps, as you know, pay the salaries of the doctors and technicians."

"Wait just one minute," I said. "Yes, doctors are experimenting with new drugs. How else would we come up with medications to fight all these horrible illnesses? You're understandably upset, Edith, but we have no idea what the problem might be. Come down to the office and let me run some tests."

After a short hesitation she said nonchalantly, "I have a purple tumor on my leg. Every day it grows larger. It's now the size of a plum. It started as a small spot. It is just as the article describes it—Kaposi's sarcoma, they called it: classic AIDS."

The following morning Edith arrived at my office. She was a remarkably handsome eighty-year-old woman, slim and straight, in an elegant dark dress. She carried the newspaper article about AIDS in a hand bedecked by three large rings.

She had once been an English professor at a renowned women's college and still edited literary papers and books for a prestigious publishing firm. In fact, she had edited one of my own books. A vegetarian, she prided herself on her excellent health and personal grooming. Each morning she swam two miles at the local Junior High School. She lived alone, in the very house in which she was born. She boasted of being a descendant of one of the families who arrived on the Mayflower. She adamantly refused Medicare because, as she'd put it ten years earlier, "Those of us who are left with any pride don't need the government's charity. I have enough money provided by my ancestors to take care of all medical bills, including yours."

Years ago she left a living will with me, which ordered that she was not to be resuscitated, nor were any heroic measures to be used in the event of a fatal illness. In fact, she was one of the early members of the Hemlock Club, advocates of an individual's right to suicide when confronted with a terminal illness.

Sitting opposite me, she appeared fatigued and sickly for the first time in years.

"This article is badly written, but at least it describes this terrible disease. You should read it, Doctor. I will leave it with you. Maybe it will give you an idea for another book, a real book. Why don't you write a book about real people like me, what they feel, what you feel? You have a thousand stories as a doctor. Everybody pities the ill, but few understand them."

Though she could be intimidating, Edith enchanted me.

"Edith, you have often come to me with bizarre symptoms and then made your own diagnosis and prognosis. This time, please, with your gracious permission, allow me to examine you and perform some pertinent tests."

"You know me well enough, Doctor. I have not missed a diagnosis in years. That's more than I can say for you. But go ahead and play doctor and then tell me about your next book, which should be more productive than simply listening to an old hag."

"Edith, there are ten people out there waiting for their appointments. I don't have time to fence with you. Let's get on with it."

"Of course, if you are too busy, Herr Professor, I can go

elsewhere. There was a time when you sat around and lis-
tened to patients. Now it's all business. The price of success,
no doubt. In and out of your office—next patient!"

I tried very hard to restrain myself. Edith was an old
friend and a dear person, though clearly today she was going
to be a nuisance.

"I have not seen you for a year, Edith. When did all this
start?"

"Nine months ago, to be exact. I remember that day
because I had just returned from Africa."

She took out a small pad which was filled with dozens of
pages of notes in a neatly written hand.

"Are you going to read that whole book to me?" I asked.

"Don't worry, good doctor, I just want to be sure I have
the chronology correct. To summarize, my first symptom was
fatigue. As you may recall, I am up at five every morning, do
my Air Force exercises, then have a light breakfast and read
the *New York Times*. By eight o'clock I open the school pool
and swim my laps. A few months ago, I began to feel tired
by the tenth lap, which I attributed to my age, and I simply
reduced the number of laps. But I started to become more
and more fatigued each day, and soon I lost my appetite and
began to lose weight. I developed one miserable cold after
another and then the coughing started. I had no fever."

"Did you take your temperature?" I asked.

"You know damn well I don't keep a thermometer in the
house. I can tell if I am running a fever."

She stopped speaking for a second and then began to
cough, a dry, violent spasm that caused her to lose her breath.
I handed her a cup of water.

"I am concerned about that cough," I said with deep
concern. You may be suffering from pneumonia. Please go
on with your symptoms."

"Well, I noticed one morning that my neck was as swollen

as a walrus's. I could feel dozens of little devilish glands in my neck. That convinced me I had AIDS: weakness, coughing, loss of appetite, swollen glands. It's got to be AIDS, right?"

"Or a hundred other diseases, Edith. But before you kill yourself, give me your body first," I said with a wink.

"Very funny, but nothing works anymore. There isn't a single organ that could be recycled. Not one, not even, well, maybe one…Just because I look like an old hag doesn't mean my sex life hasn't been active. Don't look so shocked. We old-timers have the same feelings as you do. Our hormones are still there; the level may be down, but what's left is plenty. You just have to keep the juices flowing. You know the saying: 'Use it or lose it.' I have never been married, but I have been mistress of many famous men. My four-poster bed has been warmed by some of the best. Now I am afraid one of them did me in, and I think I know who the slob is—a lousy accountant, but he was so charming! We sacked up for a winter. Then I found out that the creep also liked little boys, and that he is dying of AIDS. So there it is."

Edith did unravel me with her story. Through all those years, doctoring her for benign complaints, she had always left with me the impression that she was a staid conservative Victorian woman who spent her days reading and munching on carrots. She proceeded to make a list for me of her former lovers, which included artists and other prominent men she had met during her long stays in Vienna and Berlin in the 1920s. I took a long, slow look at her.

Her fine profile and her demeanor reminded me of Marlene Dietrich, the love of my youthful fantasies. Now when I stared into her blue eyes, I thought I saw, for the first time, the naughty eyes of a sensuous old woman. Perhaps she was indeed a victim of this new scourge. If she did turn out to be afflicted with AIDS, she would be the oldest woman recorded to have it. Hardly a distinction she would covet.

My nurse escorted her into the examining room and gave her a gown. When I entered she was sitting on the examining table, fully dressed, the gown on her lap.

"Edith, I can't examine you with your clothes on."

"There is no need to examine me. Just order the necessary tests and I will be on my way. You can charge me your usual fee and I won't say anything. Write in your notes that you performed a complete examination, etc. etc. Who the hell will know?"

"Edith, I have to listen to your lungs."

"You don't have to. Just order an X-ray."

"At least let me listen to your heart."

"You don't have to. Just do an EKG."

"Edith, an EKG doesn't tell me everything about your heart."

"Well, that's fine, then, you don't have to do an EKG."

"I need to examine your abdomen to see if there are any enlargements, tumors, or—"

She interrupted me again. "Order an X-ray. I am not afraid of radiation. It is more accurate, anyway, and I am not going into the hospital, either, to be on display for your students, no matter how sick I get. I have the right to refuse any treatment, and I certainly have the right to refuse to be hospitalized."

It was impossible for me to tame her cantankerousness. My only choice would be to refer her to another physician.

"If you want to see another physician, by all means do," I told her in a voice full of frustration and anger.

"You mean to say that you don't want to take care of me?"

"I did not say that. I just find it difficult to make a proper diagnosis or to give you adequate care under these conditions, your conditions."

"It is my right," she insisted. "Take it or leave it." Her blue eyes bored into me.

Traditional practice of medicine involves the careful examination of the patient, looking for hidden clues that will lead the doctor to a diagnosis—a correct one, we hope. Like Sherlock Holmes, we were trained to solve mysteries by step-by-step inductions, through rational analysis of seemingly disconnected and irrelevant facts. Alas, those wonderful days of medical sleuthing are all but over. Sophisticated testing has replaced much of the traditional art of medicine. Physical diagnosis based on the art of personal examination of a patient has become a weak sister in medical education. Although I lament the bygone days of bedside clinical diagnosis, I recognize that we save more lives today with our brilliant tests that confirm what we suspect than we would if we relied solely on our physical findings.

Edith finally allowed me to examine her thin neck. It was filled with enlarged lymph glands, which felt like a bunch of hardened grapes. She raised her dress above her bony knees and then slowly pulled down the black stocking covering her left leg. Mounted on the lower part of her leg was the purple tumor. It was round, soft, ugly, a red ring around its neck. It was clearly Kaposi's sarcoma, a tumor I had seen only twice, at a former leper colony in Paris long ago.

"Well, are you convinced? It has been growing on my body for eight months. It is so horrible-looking. It is like something alive that is eating me, taking my body away."

"We can't be sure," I told Edith in a resigned but desperate voice. "We have to do a biopsy, and if it is a sarcoma, it will respond dramatically to treatment. But it doesn't necessarily mean you have AIDS." I couldn't imagine why she had waited so long to come to me.

The initial blood tests disclosed that she was severely anemic, which explained, at least in part, her weakness. She would need a blood transfusion. She did not appear anemic because her diaphanous skin was always pale; she had protected it from the sun all her life.

Back in my consulting room, Edith sat listlessly, waiting for the verdict, the diagnosis that was going to determine her future. But I had none to give her, except speculative causes for her anemia, the hideous grapes in her neck, and the heinous growth on her leg.

"Edith, you need to be transfused," I told her. "Aren't you short of breath? Doesn't your heart pound?"

"I will not get transfused," she said with a loud, imperious voice. "I don't want to get AIDS from someone else's blood."

"But you think you already have AIDS."

"That is different. I don't want another dose of AIDS from some poor devil afflicted like me. And, yes, I am short of breath, thank you."

It was pointless to pursue this conversation. Edith had her preconceived ideas, and this octogenarian rebel was determined to control her own fate.

"Edith, can I at least ask you some medical questions to help me plan some strategy for medical care?"

"Go ahead. I will cooperate up to a point." She opened a bag, pulled out some wool and needles, and began to knit.

"There is no sense wasting time. I can answer your questions better if I knit, like Madame Defarge. You do know who that is, my literate doctor? Remember her?"

"Have you been at all breathless in the past few weeks?" I asked, ignoring her taunt.

"Yes."

"Have you had palpitations?"

"Yes."

"Any weakness of your arms or legs?"

"Yes to both; and numbness, terrible numbness in both legs. My legs feel like someone placed iron shackles on them. I drop things and, Doctor, you will be happy to hear, I gave up smoking because I kept dropping the bloody cigarette."

She continued on and on, enumerating more symptoms: dragging her legs, seeing double when watching TV, suffering constant ruthless headaches.

"But you seem to be able to knit all right."

"Not really," she answered. If you were more observant, you would see I am doing most of the stitches improperly."

"How is your memory, Edith?" I asked.

"Failing rapidly, I am sorry to say. I have lost words, Doctor. I confuse objects. I know what they are, but I call them something else. And it isn't senility. I have read all about that. It's more like Alzheimer's disease in the early stages."

Maybe not so early, I thought. There were still no tests to perform for Alzheimer's. It was a diagnosis made only when other possibilities had been excluded. She cleverly covered up her memory loss with evasive tactics. For example, when I asked who was currently president, she answered, "You know, it's been the same old man for years. Why do you ask me such a silly and obvious thing?"

The minimal mental testing I performed did show that she had definite mental impairment, as evidenced by recent memory loss. She had lost the ability to retain new facts and had forgotten some past events. AIDS can cause the brain to become like Swiss cheese, and the symptoms can resemble Alzheimer's.

I could see the anguish on Edith's wrinkled face. She began to sob pitifully, an agonizing heart-rending sob.

"What I feared the most," she breathlessly spoke through her tears, "is happening to me. I thought I could beat it all: cancer, heart disease, anything. I never dreamed such a disgusting disease would get me and cause my brain to go. My brain, my memory, my intellect—nothing else matters! My father once said to me, 'Nobody can take away what you carry in your head.' I guess that's not true. I knew something was very wrong when I began to forget telephone numbers of friends. Then I couldn't recall who wrote Madame Bovary after having taught a Flaubert course for years."

I now feared it had been a mistake to give Edith this test. Suicide rates were high among the elderly, and I did not forget Edith's commitment to the Hemlock Club.

"I want to put you in the hospital," I told her. "There is no proof at all that you are suffering from AIDS. You must let me do more tests and let me examine you. I must have a dermatological biopsy of that thing on your leg. Right now there is someone at Yale who is using an experimental drug for memory loss that does show promise."

I knew that if she left my office without agreeing to any of this, I would not see her again.

"I am the last of my family," she said sadly. "Everyone is dead and there is no reason for me to go on living."

She saw the distraught look on my face and said, not unsympathetically, "Don't look so sad, Doctor, I have had a good life. I did almost everything I wanted to. I traveled from Alaska to Zaire; tried every type of food; taught thousands of people to write and read, some of whom went on to write important books. I've slept with some of the best people under the sun, except for that damned accountant."

"Give me two weeks," I told Edith. "Two weeks to solve your problem. Then if there is no positive resolution, you can do what you wish."

Perhaps if I could strike a bargain with this difficult and recalcitrant woman, I would prevent her from killing herself. She eyed me with a surreptitious glance and then, to my shock, simply said, "Agreed. I owe you that much after twenty years of bothering you."

The following day I was pleasantly surprised when one of the blood tests returned, indicating that she was suffering from pernicious anemia, which can occur in vegetarians

who don't supplement their diet with B12. Pernicious ane-
mia causes all the symptoms that Edith exhibited: weakness,
gland swelling, numbness of the extremities, weight and
memory loss, and shortness of breath.

I told Edith the good news, and the following day she
arrived, her face sparkling with happiness, but still dragging
her foot like a chained prisoner from Devil's Island.

"So, you solved my problem, you wonderful doctor."

"We need to give you weekly B12 shots, and then
monthly. That will take care of the anemia, and your numb-
ness will improve, as will as the dragging of your foot."

"And my memory?"

"That, too, should get better."

"How simple. Modern medicine is miraculous, and I gave
you such a difficult time. Of course, anemia can cause all of
this. I will get another chance. Thank you, Doctor."

I know of no greater satisfaction under the sun than to
make a patient feel better and then to hear those three rare
and precious words.

All went well for a while. The anemia was improving rapidly
but, to my dismay, the leg did not improve. But, euphoric over
her general improvement, Edith paid less and less attention
to her dragging foot. She no longer worried about an AIDS
diagnosis because her strength had returned. Sometimes
pernicious anemia can cause irreversible nerve damage.

At the end of six weeks, Edith's euphoria, at first a loud
and brilliant symphony, began to fade to a distant bell as the
other leg became affected. She stumbled around her home
like a drunken sailor, laboriously navigating her body from
sofa to chair to bathroom, using the furniture as support.

"I am no better!" she cried over the phone. "You lied to
me, and I thought you were my friend, my only friend."

She still refused hospitalization and a biopsy, but she did

consent to see a neurologist, who diagnosed her as having a degenerative disease of the nervous system. The CT scan of the brain was normal, and we awaited results from an AIDS test. But her leg tumor was enlarging. She kept it well concealed under dark stockings.

Now confined to a wheelchair, requiring twenty-four-hour nursing at home, Edith saw her worst fears coming true. Her speech became slurred and her vision began to fail, along with her other faculties. I visited her at home and she finally agreed to be admitted into the hospital.

She lived in a charming brownstone in the old section of town, which hadn't been turned into parking lots, pizza parlors, or video stores. Luckily, she had sufficient money to pay for the homecare she needed; otherwise, she would have been doomed to a nursing home.

The large living room was like an overstuffed Victorian parlor, replete with sumptuous red sofas, large pillows, and original paintings by well-known artists, which she had collected during her stay in Berlin. Everywhere were works of art, from pre-Columbian fertility statues to early Picasso figurines. Her home was a museum, a treasure that reflected her life.

A generous library covered one entire wall, and on another was a long antique hunt table covered with hundreds of pictures from Edith's life. Dozens of photos displayed her standing with interesting-looking men in different parts of the world. I couldn't recognize the accountant among them. In one, she was standing with another woman and three men in Nazi uniforms. I recognized Albert Speer, architect of the Third Reich. The two other men wore the uniforms of the Reichsführer; they were group leaders in the SS.

"I see you found those pictures fast enough. I am not proud of those," she said. "I know you were one of the lucky ones who escaped. Can I offer you a book to drink?" she asked.

I waited for her to correct herself.

"You know, Doctor, I have to return to the U.S. I don't like what I see here in Berlin."

"You are in the U.S., Edith," I said softly.

"I know where I am! How dare you, Doctor, infer that I am mad? Please call my brother, Leo, immediately and tell him I must speak to him."

Leo had died ten years earlier. She had shared an apartment with him in Berlin.

"Edith, you are not well. I am going to take you to the hospital so we can make you better," I said.

"All right," she answered in a resigned and very old voice.

I looked at this woman, once a grand a lady, now sitting helplessly in a wheelchair, frightened, alone, having arrived almost at the very end of her long, illustrious life. The days ahead would be marked by a long series of tests in the hospital and daily needle pricks. After tens of thousands of dollars' worth of hospitalization, and the humiliation and pain, she might still be dumped in a convalescent home to die alone.

From her home, I made arrangements for Edith's hospital admission, no easy task because of the acute shortage of nursing staff then. Because I declared Edith to be an emergency case, she had to go to the emergency room first to be screened by the resident, who would have to approve her admission.

"What is the diagnosis?" the resident asked me on the phone.

"It might be AIDS."

An alarm bell went off in the resident's head, which triggered a chain of precautions.

I accompanied her to the hospital, where the staff wore masks and gloves when they greeted her. Edith was placed in a private room with full infectious-disease precautions, especially because she was coughing.

"Am I that sick that I have to be isolated? Why don't they burn my house down?" she screamed. "Like in the days of the plague, burn the clothes and destroy all that is connected to me?"

"Edith, I am sorry, but that is the present hospital policy for anyone possibly suffering from a contagious infectious disease. As soon as the test for AIDS returns negative, the masks and gloves will be removed."

The once gregarious bon vivant was now in solitary confinement, awaiting her ultimate fate. If the AIDS test returned positive, she could look forward to a dreadful death from lung complications that would slowly take her breath away. Her entire gastrointestinal tract might become like raw meat. She would suffer intractable diarrhea, and her weight loss would continue until she looked like a concentration camp victim. Once the devastating course began, it marched forward relentlessly. Back then, there was no effective treatment to stop the grotesque progression to death. It would become a fruitless wait, as we doctors stood around watching the disease play itself out.

It wasn't so long ago that doctors used to sit by a patient's bedside, observing the natural course of a deadly illness. The similarity between the consequences of AIDS in its early years and the plague of the Middle Ages was stark.

Edith finally allowed me to examine her thoroughly. I found that she had a loud heart murmur. Her heart was as enlarged as a balloon, and her lungs rattled with water. The heart valve was destroyed, which explained her chronic cough: she was suffering from heart failure. She would have to undergo open-heart surgery to save her life. Surgeons, understandably, are reluctant to operate on people with AIDS for fear of puncturing the skin and coming into contact with the patient's blood.

With medications, her heart failure improved in forty-eight hours, her cough lessened, and the shortness of breath practically disappeared.

Each day, for a few minutes, I sat at her bedside, chatting with her as an old friend. We talked about Vienna and Berlin and Bertolt Brecht, Lotte Lehmann, and our favorite authors, Arthur Schnitzler, Stefan Zweig, and Thomas Mann, and I listened to her stories from the past.

"I feel like I am on Mann's Magic Mountain. I will have to read the book again when I can see better. The Magic Mountain at Luzerne, Switzerland, is now in New Haven, Connecticut."

She became more disoriented and drowsy, and her paralysis increased. The blood test for AIDS finally came back negative, as did others for infections of her heart. By the time I could tell her that she was not suffering from AIDS, she was into a semi-comatose state and I doubted whether she could hear me. The biopsy of the purple tumor did reveal Kaposi's sarcoma, which is not exclusively associated with AIDS. But it would have been useless to follow the oncologist's treatment plan; she was slipping away from us without our being able to understand why.

I decided to order a spinal tap, a procedure that was rarely performed anymore. I didn't want to wait for an autopsy and then wring my hands because we had missed the diagnosis. Her spinal tap was slightly abnormal and gave us the missing clue.

When Edith became oriented I told her again, with great pleasure, that she was not suffering from AIDS.

"Are you sure?" she asked me in a dubious tone. It really isn't AIDS?"

"No, it is not AIDS, but it's—"

"Let me guess," she said, reverting to her usual tone. "I caught a rare tropical illness while I was in Africa."

"No, Edith. Actually, you have brain syphilis, which is rare."

"Syphilis! How disgusting!" she said.

Then she became angry. "Who could have been responsible? Who was the pig?" she muttered.

She pulled a black leather book from a shopping bag on the floor next to her. It was a diary, or "Memoirs of My Past Adventures," as she put it.

"I wonder which one of these great men is the culprit? They're all dead now, like everybody else I knew. It doesn't really matter, does it? What a relief that it wasn't the accountant! Maybe I even gave syphilis to him."

When the treatment for her sexually transmitted disease had been completed, the paralysis miraculously improved and almost disappeared. She was able to negotiate around her room, still with a pronounced limp but fully active. Her heart, though, remained severely damaged, the valve having been destroyed. Her ankles began to swell again and her breathing became labored.

I explained to Edith that she needed open-heart surgery, that it was major surgery, that there was a five percent chance of not recovering, and that without the surgery she could not live a year.

"I guess I have no choice."

As I was about to leave the room, she said to me, "'Goodbye, my darling, I will see you tomorrow.' You know who said that?"

I looked at her in total ignorance.

"Those were the last words that Noel Coward uttered to his friends before he died."

The following morning, she underwent successful open-heart surgery. But shortly thereafter, she lapsed into a deep coma and did not recover. An autopsy disclosed that she had ruptured an aneurysm, a complication of the brain syphilis.

I would miss my colorful, cantankerous old patient more than I could have imagined.

THE INGRID BERGMAN NUN

1980

THE MORNING BEFORE I LEFT NEW ENGLAND WITH MY wife and two children for a winter holiday in St. Thomas, Sister Marian pulled me aside in the corridor of the Catholic hospital as I was conducting rounds.

"I hear you are going for some weeks to the Islands. How nice," she said.

Sister Marian was a tall, stunningly attractive woman with a persuasive way about her. We had always liked each other. She was the principal of one of the Catholic schools and also assistant to the director of the hospital. She ran both the hospital and school with an iron hand.

"We have a school on St. Thomas, high up on a hill. You could do us a big favor," she continued. "Would you mind visiting our teachers and sort of seeing if all is well?"

"Of course, I'd be glad to."

The next morning my family and I left for this beautiful jewel of an island rimmed by volcanic mountains and surrounded by the blue Caribbean, which changes color from deep blue to turquoise to sparkling emerald green. We checked into one of dozens of lookalike brown wooden condominiums facing the sea.

The following morning I rented a jeep and headed for

the Catholic church in the mountains. Up there the bustling sounds of the city were barely audible.

It was delightfully warm at nine o'clock in the morning. The sky looked like a blue painted ceiling, and the air was filled with the sweet odor of gardenias. Dressed in khaki shorts, a white short-sleeve shirt, white shoes, and a Panama hat, a stethoscope dangling from my back pocket, I felt like Dr. Schweitzer as I drove up the twisting road. Perched on the edge of the mountain, houses appeared as if they all would tumble into the sea.

The stone Catholic church, painted all white, stood majestically high on a ridge, facing the Caribbean. Sweet gentle sounds of church bells tolling the hour echoed through the mountains. On the spacious manicured lawn of the convent, five young women in swimsuits were sunning themselves. I was a bit startled by this sight.

As I approached, I was greeted by two large German shepherds, who ran up to the gate barking viciously at me. Keeping a safe distance, I yelled in what I hoped was a strong convincing voice, "Hello, I am the doctor from the U.S. and I bring greetings from Sister."

The young women ignored me and did not make any attempt to cover themselves. After a moment, I heard a familiar voice calling to me.

"Welcome to St. Mary School, Doctor."

I turned around and saw a young woman standing at the gate smiling at me. This could not be the same woman I knew from the hospital, I thought.

"Sister Marian?" I asked as I approached the gate.

"Yes, Doctor, it's me."

Seeing her dressed in comfortable island clothing, I was taken aback. In her late thirties, she was at least ten years older than the sunbathing teachers on the lawn, but far more attractive. She had the same provocative smile and elegant presence of Ingrid Bergman in *The Nun's Story*. My stare seemed to make her uncomfortable. She moved her hands to rearrange her skirt and said, "Well, dear doctor, you look surprised to see me. I decided I needed a little vacation. I'm so glad you came today. One of our senior sisters is very ill and is running a fever."

Sister Marian opened the gate.

"Just follow me, Doctor. Sister Louise is upstairs in bed."

We climbed the narrow stairs to the third floor. In the hallway lit only by a small ceiling lamp, I could hardly see the numbered oak doors. What a striking contrast between the sepulchral scene here and the one outside in the blazing sun.

Sister Louise was covered with several tattered army blankets pulled up to her head of disheveled gray hair. Her pale sickly face stared at me. After Sister Marian introduced me, the old woman said, "We are blessed," in a soft mousy voice. She withdrew a wrinkled hand from under the blankets to shake mine.

I suddenly felt uncomfortable in my shorts and polo shirt, but they did not seem to bother the nuns.

"How do you feel, Sister?" I asked as I sat down on the bed next to her and felt her racing pulse.

"I am so cold and I can't stop shivering," she replied. "What a devoted doctor you are to come my aid."

After I examined her lungs with Sister Marian standing by, I was certain she was suffering from pneumonia. Back home I would have sent her straight to the hospital, but she refused to go to the local one here, which had a reputation of substandard care.

The sisters, however, were very resourceful. Their medicine chest was stacked with all the supplies most hospitals have on hand. I gave instructions on how to care for the patient, then I said goodbye and found my way back outside.

It was good to feel the hot sun and fresh breezes of the

islands again after departing from the sick bed of a pneumonia patient. Prior to this I'd held the traditional image of nuns clothed to the neck in traditional black or white habits, but as I drove down the mountain I kept picturing all those sisters, who were teachers in the Catholic school, lounging almost naked on the lawn.

My family was preparing for a day of sailing. My wife was used to these interruptions, either in the middle of the night or even on an airplane when a medical emergency arose.

"I'm glad at least that you don't have your beeper with you," she said.

I took my wife and two daughters sailing. Suddenly the sky darkened and a sharp wind billowed our sails. I tried not to show my panic, as I knew we were in danger of capsizing, far from shore. We arrived safely back and my wife said, "Thank you, whoever is up there." She turned to me and remarked, "Perhaps the nuns prayed for our safety."

That evening, we went to bed early. I was dreaming about sailing, with the young nuns in their bathing suits swimming alongside us like dolphins, when the phone rang and I awoke abruptly. I placed a pillow over my head and ignored it, but it would not stop ringing.

"Darling, answer the damn phone so we can all get some sleep," my wife said.

I picked it up and once again heard Sister Marian's voice. "Doctor, I know it is terrible to awaken you at four in the morning. God forgive me, but my heart is racing so fast. It started a while ago, and here on the island we have no way to get to the hospital at this hour. What should I do?"

I learned long ago that you don't ignore a rapid heart and a frightened patient. I reassured her that I was on my way.

"I have to go, dear," I told my wife as I got out of bed. "One of the sisters at the convent is having palpitations."

"What did the convent do before you came here?" my wife wondered.

The night on this delightful island can bring a smile and a sigh to the coldest heart. The same trade winds that brought Columbus to this part of the world blew a soft breeze from the east. The darkness of the night was lit up by a mysterious moon complementing the sparkling stars. I could clearly see Venus glowing and the Big Dipper and the North Star. Pollution from the hundreds of cruise ships had not yet blanketed this magnificent night sky.

On the mountain I beheld a wondrous view. The roads were lit up by the silver moonlight, and the city lights below looked like Fifth Avenue at Christmastime. I had never made a house call surrounded by such radiance. And I had certainly never made a house call to a church to render medical care to a nun at four in the morning.

Some interior lights were lit in the convent, which created an eerie scene. Two of the teachers were waiting for me at the gate, this time wearing bathrobes.

"Thank God you came," the younger one said. They led me into the convent, up the narrow stairs to a darkened hallway and into room number 1. Sister Marian was lying in the small narrow bed looking pale and sullen. She looked at me with fear in her beautiful eyes. The walls of the sick room were painted white, a simple two-drawer pine wood night table stood next to the bed with a candle and a Bible. An old-fashioned porcelain bedpan was sticking out of the bottom shelf of the night stand. Three nuns were standing watch like guardian angels. It was a setting from another century. If the calendar matched my surroundings, I would be wearing a black morning coat with a stiff white collar, my stethoscope would be a wooden tube, and I would be pulling the bedpan out to examine the urine.

Sister Marian looked up at me and spoke softly, "My

heart is racing. I am not prepared to meet my maker yet. Should I call the priest to give me last rites?" she asked.

I sat down on the bed next to her and took her hand. The pulse was rapid but regular.

"Not yet, Sister Marian, let me use my stethoscope. Will one of you ladies be good enough to help Sister off with her clothing so I can listen to her heart?"

I stepped out of the room and waited until I was called back in. They had covered her small bosom with a towel, and they scrutinized me as I moved the stethoscope around her chest, moving the towel aside. As was my habit, I closed my eyes to hear better. Sister Marian's heart was indeed racing, but I heard no murmurs.

"By the way, you wouldn't have an EKG machine around, would you?" I asked facetiously.

"We do, Doctor," Sister Marian said, covering herself with the towel. One of the sisters brought it in and attached the straps to her arms and legs and placed the metal chest leads on her bare chest as Sister Marian kept repeating how grateful she was that I had come to her aid.

"We were shown how to run the EKG machine, but not how to read it," one of the nuns said.

"We have all kinds of heart medications here if you want to use them, and we can set up an IV. We even have a defibrillator," another nun added.

I studied the EKG and announced, "It is just a fast heartbeat, Sister, not to worry. If in your little pharmacy you have some Valium, that is all that's needed, and as the sun rises you will be back to normal. If not, call me again. Just wondering, was there anything to upset you, Sister? Stress, or anything at all?"

"No, Doctor, nothing that I can think of," she replied. "Bless you, Doctor, for your kindness and expertise." As she sat up the towel fell from her chest, and I had a glimpse of her small breasts. I looked away as the younger nun swiftly covered her.

"What a sweet, charming voice that nun has," my wife said when she hung up the phone. "The medication helped her—the heart palpitation disappeared, the sister wanted to tell you."

One week later, two days before leaving our paradise island, my family and I were tanned and rested but had no desire to return to the cold gray skies of New England. We made plans to take a day trip to St. John—an island off the coast to be reached by a twenty-minute ferry ride—to do some snorkeling. As we were leaving our condominium apartment, the phone rang. I had a fair idea of who it might be.

I dropped the snorkeling gear and picked up the receiver. As soon as I said hello, I heard the unmistakable voice of Sister Marian speaking softly.

"I am not calling about me," she said, "but the bishop of the Virgin Islands. He heard of the excellent care you rendered to the sisters and to me, and he wondered if you would give a quick listen to his heart, which he said was skipping. He will be glad to come to your place."

I put my hand over the receiver and explained things to my wife.

"Go ahead. I will explain to the children," she said. "How can you refuse a Bishop? I never realized that the U.S. Virgin Islands had a bishop." The families of doctors grow accustomed to taking a backseat to patients.

I told Sister Marian that I would see the bishop the next day.

Sharply at 2:00 p.m. the next day, a chauffeur drove a long black limousine up to our condominium. Sister Marian climbed out of the backseat, followed by the very tall and pallid bishop, who made a striking appearance. The

Sister was wearing her white nun's outfit, her blond hair pinned back.

As the bishop approached me, he proffered a long hand with a large ring on his third finger. Surely he did not expect me to kiss it? Instead, I shook his hand like an old acquaintance.

"Most kind of you, Doctor, to take the time out from your vacation and your family."

"Welcome, Your Reverence." I had no idea how to address him.

I escorted the bishop into a bedroom of the condo and examined him while Sister Marian waited in the living room. When I had finished, having found nothing unusual, we joined Sister Marian. The bishop asked if he might have a glass of water.

On impulse I replied, "Why not something more refreshing, like a vodka tonic?"

"Splendid idea, Doctor. I am sure Sister would not object."

His eyes gave her a soft stare. "She is welcome to join us if she wishes."

The Ingrid Bergman smile appeared on her pale face, along with a hint of a blush in her cheeks. "Of course. It would be refreshing," she said, looking a little flirtatiously first at me and then at the bishop.

The bishop rose from his chair like a giant bat and, unbuttoning his flowing black gown, walked toward the sliding door that opened onto the porch. He was struck by the cool breeze and the view of the calm sea with sailboats in the distance.

"It is like a painting, a Dufy," he announced. "No wonder Gabrielle Pissarro painted here—he was born in St. Thomas. I am certain you knew that already. He was of the Hebrew faith, Doctor, as Sister informed me. You must have visited the oldest synagogue under the American flag here in St.

Thomas."

"Oh yes, we always try to attend Friday night services," I lied. "It's a marvelous synagogue dating back to the 1840s. There is sand on the floor."

Sister Marian stayed near me in the small kitchenette. "Let me help, Doctor. You are very generous and kind to us." I opened the freezer and pulled out a bottle of vodka. She reached above the counter to fetch three glasses. I bent down to find the tonic water in the lower cabinets; as I rose, I accidentally touched her body and, to my surprise, she did not immediately draw back. Next I pulled out the ice tray and handed it to her. She removed the cubes with her fingertips and placed them in the glasses, smiling as she poured generous quantities of vodka into each one. She carried two glasses to the veranda and handed one to the bishop. I followed her, and we all sat down on the porch chairs.

Drinking vodka with a nun and a bishop was a new experience for me.

By the time we had finished our drinks and refilled them twice, with Sister acting as hostess, we had discussed the politics of the island and Castro. The bishop rose from his chair looking as serene as he had before, but Sister now had a red glow to her cheeks. Her voice sounded a pitch higher as I escorted them to the door.

"Sister Marian," I said almost in a whisper, "I have to tell you: you look like Ingrid Bergman, my favorite actress of all time."

"Thank you, Doctor! That is the nicest compliment I have ever received."

My wife suddenly appeared beside me as the limousine departed.

"That nun is a beautiful woman," she remarked. "She reminds me of a movie actress."

"Actually, she does look like Ingrid Bergman, now that you mention it," I replied.

Two weeks later, back home in New England, my tan may have been fading, but the memory of Sister Marian and the bishop lingered. I did not run into her at the hospital for a few months, but when I did she asked if she could see me as soon as possible. I told her to come in the following morning and she arrived early, wearing her traditional nun's outfit and looking very serious. Her blue eyes were anxious and frightened.

"I have a favor to ask of you," she whispered. "This is most confidential."

She moved her chair closer to the desk and bent her body as if to pray. I sat back in my swivel chair, not having the faintest idea what this beautiful nun was going to ask of me.

"Doctor," she began, then cleared her throat and said, "I am leaving the Order. I have given my notice. I can't lie to myself and to God. I need one more favor from you. I know it sounds terribly vain, but you saw my breasts. They are so small, and I want to have them enlarged. Can you please refer me to a plastic surgeon, the best one you know?"

I kept a poker face. She must have fallen in love, I suspected, but with whom? Could it be the bishop? I also wondered how a young beautiful woman could decide to enter the Order in the first place. I couldn't ask for answers to any of these questions, but I did ask her how long she had been in the Order.

"Five years and ten days, Doctor."

I gave her the name of a good plastic surgeon and wished her well. A patient of mine had recently undergone the procedure, so I was able to tell her that it would cost three thousand dollars. Sister Marian nodded, gave me her Ingrid

Bergman smile, and left my office. I was never to see her again.

A few weeks later I received a visit from Sister Louise, the elderly nun I had treated on St. Thomas.

"I need something to calm my nerves, Doctor," she said. "I took charge of the school after dear Sister Marian left the Order. It is a very difficult job for me."

She hesitated, then spoke again with tears in her eyes. "And to make matters worse, a terrible thing has happened in our convent. Someone stole three thousand dollars from the coffers. It has left us in terrible straits."

The *NOCTURNAL* *GARDENER*

1990

WHEN I FIRST MET BILL HE WAS WEARING A DARK SUIT, a white button-down shirt, and a blue striped tie. He was a tall young man with a pale face and eyes as black as coal. During the day he was employed by a computer firm, but his real ambition was to be a gardener, to own a landscape business. He responded to my want ad in the local newspaper.

"I need a gardener, a caretaker, someone to clean up the place, cut the grass, and plant flowers, beautiful flowers," I told him. "I used to take care of the grounds myself, but I got tired of it. And my garden never seemed to thrive quite the way I wanted it to." The job was his.

For the first of his weekly visits, he arrived near dusk in a Cherokee Jeep driven by a young woman. She was tall and slender with long brown hair. She had the delicate features of a gently carved Grecian goddess. She carried with her a small book, which she never opened. The two, side by side, holding hands, could have been posing for one of Picasso's blue period paintings.

"I will wait for you until you are finished," I heard her say in a gentle voice. She handed him a piece of fruit and a small canteen. "It is very warm. You must drink water if you sweat too much; otherwise you will feel weak."

He kissed her on the lips and made his way to the tool-shed. She sat in the jeep, patiently waiting for him in the darkness.

"Why work at night, and so late?" I asked him.

"It is cooler and the ground is soft and moist at night. It makes digging and planting easier." Each time he came, his girlfriend sat in the Cherokee Jeep quietly.

He did a splendid job, this nocturnal gardener of mine. Once while a dangerous thunderstorm soaked the earth, which was dry from weeks of torrid heat, he continued digging, unperturbed.

From my window, I saw him place the garden tools in the shed, raise his head to the sky to catch the rain in his opened mouth, and then walk over to the jeep. The young woman wiped his face and hair with a towel as if he'd just stepped out of a shower. As he backed out of the driveway, she placed her slender arms around his wet body, her lips on his cheek.

They hardly spoke, but her eyes were always fastened on him.

He planted flowers that I had never seen before. Soon my garden gleamed with a kaleidoscope of rich colors. He looked with pride upon his work, like an artist. Each week he presented me with a modest bill and made suggestions about how to beautify the grounds.

"You have a charming young friend," I told him. "She is welcome to rest inside while you work. She need not sit out there alone in the dark."

"No, she likes to sit in the jeep and listen to the wind and the trees."

I waited eagerly for the gardener to come just to catch a glimpse of her. She would drive the jeep to the far side of the driveway, then tie a red bandanna around his head, adjusting it carefully so it did not cover his eyes.

"You must come during the day sometimes, to see the colors of the garden," I told the young woman. "Your boyfriend did such a splendid job."

"Yes, he does it with love. It is his way. I don't have to see the flowers. I can feel and smell the flowers, especially at night when the fragrance is so much keener. But perhaps one day I will come in daylight."

"Are you a student?" I asked. I knew she did not want to speak to me, but I persisted. I wasn't lonely, though I lived alone at the time, but she intrigued me. "You look like an art student or an English major."

"Neither. I work as a receptionist at the place where my boyfriend works," she replied. "I used to go to school," she added proudly, unashamed that now she was a receptionist in the computer company just to be near her lover. I couldn't help picturing her posed in the garden like a nude Aphrodite statue.

On one night when the cold and warm air met, a thick fog enveloped my house. A full moon reflected eerie shadows on the garden. It was late, and I surrendered to the night and to my bed alone. I was sure the lovers were not coming when I saw the lights of the jeep streaming through the fog. I looked through the window and witnessed a beautiful scene unfolding.

She undressed in the darkness, in the moonlight, and her naked feet danced among the flowers. She raised her long slender arms to the moon. I caught a glimpse of her radiant body in the shimmering light. She became a goddess of the night, and her lover was now at her side; he placed flowers from the garden in her hair. They never touched. When the dance was over and she tiptoed back to his jeep, the gardener followed. The jeep moved out of the driveway, leaving behind the vestiges of magic.

For days the vision unnerved me. Had I dreamed it? Perhaps the garden now did have magical power that this strange beautiful woman brought to it.

Days passed and I did not see the gardener. At first I became annoyed, then anger gave way to melancholy. At least he should have had the decency to call if he no longer wanted to work, I thought.

He did not even bother to collect his salary. Each night I waited, canceling my own plans just to sit by the window looking, waiting. Sleepless nights followed one after another. The image of the young woman dancing naked in the garden never left me.

Finally, I relinquished my pride and made the call. The gardener answered the phone in his usual ethereal voice.

"I will be there tomorrow, Doctor, I promise," he said. "I was tied up a little." No apologies, no explanations. It was not important enough for him to give any explanations to an old man.

He arrived in the middle of the morning the next day. "Where is your girlfriend?" I asked with consternation in my voice.

I wanted to tell him how I had watched their moonlight dance, and how the garden had become special, magical, by her touch, her breath on the flowers.

He must have sensed my disappointment.

"We broke up" was all he said. He went to work in the garden with no joy.

Now he came during the day, in the torrid sun, all his movements slowed. He neglected to weed and to water, and before long the garden looked unattractive, abandoned. I dared not say anything to him. His eyes were red and swollen.

He was moving as if in a dream, going through the

motions of being alive.

"What happened?" I asked him.

"It just happened. One day she said she no longer wanted me."

She had done her job well, this enchanted sorceress from another world, and then disappeared.

"You are so young and there are hundreds of women out there for you to meet," I said. But I knew that there is only one real love. I, too, felt his loss.

Several weeks later I asked him to trim the bushes around the house. He refused the electric cutter and used an old pair of garden scissors. He worked at a feverish pace, sweating profusely, snipping as if he were cutting the pain from his heart. He worked in silence, rounding out all the bushes in perfect symmetry like a compulsive draftsman, completely oblivious to throngs of hornets circling his head. Then suddenly he straightened his bent body, flinching with pain from the dozens of bites. He dropped the scissors, desperately slapping hornets from his face and neck.

"Doctor," he called in a soft, hollow voice, "can I see you for a minute?"

I was in my study, angry at the young man for being so nonchalant, so indifferent to a lost love. Not a word of regret. Did he not miss her, as I did? Had it been just a fling for him? I slowly approached the porch door in response.

"Some hornets bit me and I'm allergic to them."

He looked frightened and his face was the color of mud. I rushed to the medicine cabinet and found some Benadryl, which he gulped down with water.

"How do you feel?"

"Not so good. My lips are swelling, and my mouth feels like it is filled with cotton."

Right before my eyes his arms and face became reddened and swelled up as if someone had inflated a red balloon. His body swayed like a drunken sailor's as I guided him to the backseat in my car.

"We have to hurry," I said. "There is not much time." I knew that an allergic reaction this intense could soon be fatal.

I drove through traffic lights, beeping the horn, swinging my stethoscope out of the window so cars would make way for me as I sped desperately to the emergency room. In the mirror I could see his ashen face.

"How are you? Keep talking," I said to him, as if speaking could help him stay alive.

"I can't breathe, I feel something heavy on my chest, everything is dark now, like someone put a mask over my face."

I slammed on the brakes, jumped out of the car and into the backseat, breathed into his mouth, and thumped on his chest. The gardener stirred. One shot of adrenalin and he would be saved. But I had no adrenalin in the doctor's bag that lay covered with dust in the trunk of my car. That brown alligator bag given to me the day I started practice used to be part of my professional dress. Once stuffed with medicines to save lives, it had grown musty from years of disuse, the drugs browned with decay.

An ambulance might have taken ten, even fifteen minutes to arrive. He might have died by his magical garden that he had planted so lovingly. I ran back into the driver's seat, and minutes later we were in the emergency room. I screamed into the hall, a scream of despair.

"I have a dying boy in my car! He was bitten by a swarm of hornets."

They carried him to the special room for patients in cardiac arrest. My job was done. Now physicians as young as the gardener were racing to save him. How swiftly they moved, what expert reflexes, not one motion wasted. I stood there feeling helpless.

I called his mother, who at first did not understand. "Better come to the emergency room at once," I said. "Things are not going well."

"I don't drive," she said. "I will have to call his friend to take me there."

When she arrived, his mother appeared as a copy of her son, the same eyes, the same poetic face, even the same black hair. At first I was not sure if the young woman with her was the same one I'd seen dancing in the moonlight. Again she carried a book with her. She sat in the waiting room, her face motionless, not a tinge of sadness across it. She had come as the driver and nothing more.

"He knows he is allergic to bees," she said to me when she finally spoke. "He always carries the antidote with him. It's in his jeans pocket now."

And so it was. But we came across it too late to save him.

I'M FINE
1999

have survived a car-totaling accident in Switzerland, a near-shipwreck in the North Sea, and a flaming plane crash into a frozen New England lake. Not long after that last disaster, I woke in the middle of the night to find my house burning down around me; I got away with only minutes to spare. A few years later came a bitter divorce.

I had a quiet spell that lasted for many years, then came what turned out to be my most harrowing experience yet.

I was a very fit sixty-eight-year-old, an ardent tennis player, swimmer, and hiker. And as a heart doctor, I have always practiced what I preach: I don't smoke, my weight is just right, and my lipids and blood pressure are the envy of my patients. Moreover, every day I take baby aspirin and two glasses of red Bordeaux. (Not together!) I had a balanced lifestyle, a reasonable level of stress, a busy social calendar, an enjoyable practice, and a wonderful fiancée.

The previous summer we'd taken a glorious trip to Paris and France's chateau country. Indeed, things were going almost too well. But soon after we returned, that changed. When playing my daily tennis match, I got sloppy; I couldn't chase the ball. Then, during rounds, I felt exhausted while climbing my usual five flights of stairs. I was even short of breath while gardening.

Clearly something was up. A flu? Lyme disease? Asthma? Heart trouble? After wheezing my way through a whole morning of patient visits, I went to see Dr. Roth, an internist and a colleague, and asked him to check my lungs.

The chest X-ray and ECG were normal. Through his stethoscope, though, Roth heard an accentuated second sound; he suspected either coronary artery occlusion or a pulmonary embolism.

I was whisked to the radiology department for a spiral CT scan of my lung and stunned to hear the result from the chief of radiology: "You're going to have to stay with us, my friend. You have multiple pulmonary emboli."

Although my medical side understood that these blood clots in the lung could prove fatal at any moment, I was still thinking like a well person. "I have a full afternoon scheduled," I told him. "Let's wait until tomorrow." I smiled. "I'm fine."

Fortunately, my doctors knew when to overrule a patient. They placed me on a stretcher, still wearing my business clothes and tie. My office and fiancée were notified, and I was soon en route to the intensive care unit. Along the way, I hid my face behind a copy of the New York Times, like a Mafioso dodging the camera. Despite my mounting anxiety about my condition, I was also embarrassed about being carried into the ICU, where I'd be joining some of my own patients.

So when I recognized a passing nurse, I cracked a joke: "I'm making afternoon rounds from a stretcher; it's more comfortable." That meant, "I'm still one of you." But I wasn't. I was moving deeper and deeper into the country of the ill.

The signs multiplied rapidly. Soon I got the costume— one of those depressing hospital gowns, so disconcertingly amorphous. And then accoutrements appeared: I acquired an IV line in one arm, circle pads on my chest hooking me to a monitor, wires on my finger, and nasal prongs on my nose.

I was desperate to urinate but too embarrassed to tell the aide, whom I knew. Luckily, my fiancée, Lana's, arrived. Though I could see she was shocked by the news of my condition, her presence relaxed me somewhat. I asked her to help me get to the bathroom. As I struggled to stand upright, my wires got tangled. Somebody asked a nurse to bring a urinal to me instead.

Soon I was peeing in bed, lying down, in front of an audience—quite customary in my new country, but strange to me. And still I told myself, "I'm fine." I was put on heparin, a blood thinner to help dissolve the clots. An intern showed up, took a full medical history, and gave me a physical. Then she said, apologetically, "Now I have to perform a rectal on you, Dr. Kra." I feared what that inexperienced probing finger would do. So I gave her instructions on how to perform a painless rectal examination, which mercifully she was able to follow.

Next, my resident examined me. He asked excellent, thorough questions. I gave intelligent, thorough answers. And as we quietly reviewed the situation, I tried to ignore the terror that had started to swell inside me like a blowfish. I recited all the clinical and physical signs of a pulmonary embolism. I pointed at the specific area in my chest where a distinct sound could be heard. My words were calm, objective. But I was pointing at the blowfish.

He thanked me for my erudite dissertation, listened to my heart and lungs, ordered a tranquilizer—he'd noticed my growing anxiety—and raised the rails of my bed to full height. The tranquilizer did the trick: I became confident and relaxed, and told those gathered around me that pulmonary embolism isn't so terrible. A little heparin, a little oxygen, some bed rest. In no time, I'd be back on the tennis court. And once again I said, "I'm fine."

Then my little army of support pulled out. No one was with me three hours later when I began to feel pain such as I had never experienced. It was as if someone had come into my room in the middle of the night and thrust a knife into my chest. Each breath brought agony. Through all the accidents, fires, and divorce, I had never felt such helplessness. This time, I couldn't crawl out of a burning plane after it crash-landed, or run from a fiery house, or climb out the window of Gestapo headquarters. I couldn't move.

I wheezed like the wood stove in my study. A nurse arrived and gasped as she saw me suffering and struggling to breathe. I was coughing, too, and each spasm brought with it a cruel new pain. She called the intern, who called the resident, who called the attending. The intermittent morphine they pumped through my IV line gave hardly any relief.

I remembered that a colleague once explained that screaming stimulates a center in the brain that dulls pain. I thought to myself, "How can a physician start screaming?" I even recalled the cowboy movies I'd loved as a child—how I'd watched, mesmerized, as the hero bit a bullet while a surgeon dug into his flesh with a penknife to remove an arrow or a bullet. His girlfriend would wipe his brow and squeeze his hand.

I had no bullet. I bit into the bedsheet. And I let out a muffled scream.

The morphine hit every few hours wasn't helping. I felt an unrelenting stabbing sensation. Throughout the early morning hours, I wheezed and coughed ferociously, as I'd seen countless of my heart and asthma patients do.

The resident ordered an albuterol inhaler, and a technician handed me the plastic ventilator tube. Despite my misery, I somehow laughed—which only made me cough more—because the ventilator reminded me of the ram's horn that's sounded in temple during Jewish high holidays.

At four in the morning, a sweet Jamaican aide took my temperature, then measured my oxygen level, which had begun to drop dramatically. "How do you feel?" she asked in her delightful island accent. "I feel fine, never better," I answered, lying.

Why didn't I tell her, or anyone, the truth? My fear of death was well hidden. The fear of pain was close and real, but we doctors need the illusion of complete control. That illusion had no room for fear.

At times, my mind raced. How sweet, I thought, to be able to breathe freely, unrestrictedly—to be able to run across a tennis court, swim 100 yards, or jog down a country road. Or walk across a room, for that matter. Or speak without gasping after each word. Nothing in the world mattered to me at that moment. I didn't care what was happening in Taiwan or the Middle East, or whether Hillary Clinton would become a senator or Aetna would go bankrupt.

Later that morning, my fiancée returned. She wiped my brow and squeezed my hand. One of my old merchant marine buddies walked into my room just as I reached the height of despair. I gasped a greeting, then coughed at him for a while. He soon left.

Seeing that no relief came with intermittent morphine shots, my good doctor ordered a morphine pump, the kind that cancer patients use. Every few minutes, I could push a magic button and feel sweet relief. It became my best friend. I named the pump "Marilyn."

A pulmonary specialist, a cardiologist, a vascular specialist, and a hematologist—all longtime friends of mine—attended me. My two daughters came the following day, and my oldest, a nurse, decided to sleep in my room at night. The pain and coughing didn't seem to ease. "How do you feel? Isn't it better?" the concerned staff asked hourly.

Gasping, I answered: "I'm fine." As my brother, sister-in-law, rabbi, lawyer, and accountant began showing up, some part of me acknowledged the danger I was in, yet I continued to exclaim breathlessly to one and all, "I'm fine."

The shower of emboli didn't let up. I had multiple blood clots in my lungs that could kill me if they didn't dissolve. I was given a choice: I could take a clot-busting drug or have a filter placed in me that would prevent the clots from moving into my lungs. Either option could bring problems, I knew. The clot buster could cause bleeding into my brain, maybe a stroke. But placing the filter would require a delicate surgical procedure.

In my morphine haze, I had to make this important decision and I had to make it fast or my heart would begin to fail. I'd be in half-sleep, smiling like a demented clown.

I whispered, "The filter."

Minutes later, two burly men and two female aides rolled me to and fro on a bed sheet. They heaved me onto a stretcher, like a mackerel onto a deck. With monitors blinking and my forest of lines still attached, they steered my gurney through the great halls of the intensive care unit, as I smiled sickly at the nurses, interns, residents, aides, and newspaper deliveryman. Those who recognized me looked either astonished or sad. But I kept grinning and calling out, "I shall return," like General MacArthur.

The radiologist had a quiet voice and kind face. He explained what he was about to do. It was all gibberish to me—"Marilyn" was still keeping me calm—but I nodded in agreement. Again, with the help of four people, we did the rolling-on-the-sheet act, and I was lifted onto the cold X-ray table. I gasped both for air and from the pain. "You'll feel just a little stick, and some pulling," the radiologist explained. A nurse materialized with a clipboard and pen, and I heard an urgent whisper: "We forgot to have him sign the release!"

With a system full of morphine, I would blithely have

released all my assets to my ex-wife—or her lawyer, for that matter. So much for informed consent! I signed happily, and the radiologist expertly threaded the filter up my leg and into the vein of my heart, the inferior vena cava.

The following day, the crushing chest pain began to subside. They wheeled Marilyn out of the room. Seven days later, I left the hospital. Two weeks after that, I went back to my office, and three weeks later, I resumed playing tennis and swimming.

My consultants were still scratching their heads about the source of so many clots. The consensus was that they must have resulted from my plane ride home from Paris, as long periods of time sitting still are frequent triggers for clots. I'd taken all the precautions: aspirin before the trip, hourly walks during the flight, no alcohol, a lot of fluids. I even wore elastic stockings, as I'd done on much longer flights to Australia and Antarctica.

The network of professionals around me applauded my internist's astute examination, which probably saved my life. If I'd been a king, I wouldn't have received better, kinder care and attention from the house staff, doctors, nurses, aides, and secretaries.

Our medical system gets a lot of criticism, and of course it has problems. But as an expert on real trouble, I can attest to this: during my moment of greatest crisis, the system worked for me, start to finish. As a doctor, I'm proud. As a patient, I'm grateful—and a little humbled to have learned how easy it is, when you're frightened and hurting, to hide behind a wall of denial.

As thankful as I am for the care I received, in some ways I've been on high alert ever since. My own travails and those of the people around me have continued in waves of crisis and relief.

LANA'S LUCK
1999

F IVE DAYS AFTER MY GIRLFRIEND, LANA'S, AND I RETURNED from a glorious vacation in Bordeaux, she complained of an upset stomach. Soon she suffered vomiting and diarrhea.

"Most be something you ate on the trip," I consoled her.

Just to be sure, I called one of my gastroenterologist colleagues, who concurred and assured her that in a few days all would pass as quickly as it had come.

But Lana's continued to feel ill and enormously fatigued. The euphoria from our trip vanished as she complained of achiness all over her body.

It is not uncommon to have muscle and joint pains during and after a bout of gastrointestinal poisoning from tainted food. Her GI symptoms subsided, but were replaced with excruciating pain in her ankles and legs that made her scream in agony.

In the emergency room she had X-rays of her feet and ankles and blood tests for every common and exotic illness that can cause excruciating pain in a young, healthy woman. Lana's was in her thirties.

The rheumatologist had no answer and a neurologist also was baffled. Every one of the doctors agreed that the pain was related to the gastrointestinal disorder and would soon disappear. She received a prescription for pain and anti-inflammatory medications and was sent home to recuperate.

On the way home from the hospital, we stopped at our favorite restaurant, but we left before eating. Lana's was not well and could barely rise from her chair. She nearly collapsed in my arms on the way to the car.

She slept little that night and as the early morning light slipped into our bedroom, an angelic smile on her face turned toward me with joy.

"The pain is gone," she said.

Then she rolled over to her side of the bed and fell to the floor. "I can't move my legs!" she screamed.

She lay helpless on the floor and crawled to the bathroom while I dialed 911.

Soon the ambulance arrived and two EMTs raised her from the floor, placed her on a stretcher, and rushed her to the emergency room. She was terrified, and I tried not to let her see that I was, too.

One hour later she had a CAT scan of the brain, which was normal. All the blood tests were normal as well, except for a screening for Lyme disease. We live in suburban Connecticut. Our home stands in the woods and our flower and vegetable gardens are a veritable soup kitchen for the local deer, foxes, coyotes, and wild turkeys. Lyme disease can cause paralysis. I knew that West Nile virus was also a possibility, as was polio. A neurosurgeon was consulted, as well as a rheumatologist and another physician who performed a spinal tap, which also was normal. The more doctors who came to the emergency room to help us, the more frightened Lana's became, as none of them could arrive at a diagnosis.

As the day wore on, Lana's paralysis spread. She was now unable to move her trunk or raise her body from the bed.

Her doctor performed an electric conduction muscle test, sticking needles in Lana's muscles to determine the state of her nerve conduction. When the nerves in her legs did not respond, it was concluded that the likely diagnosis was Guillain-Barré Syndrome, a serious autoimmune disorder. Lana's was in great danger of becoming totally paralyzed and even dying.

Lana's was moved to the intensive care unit and I sat helplessly at her bedside watching the paralysis ascend to her arms and neck. She told me she was seeing double and finding it difficult to swallow. Each hour the situation became more critical. We feared that she would stop breathing.

Her tidal volume, which measures breathing abilities, began to fall and she would have to be intubated. Her blood pressure rose and her heart rate increased to 160. The death rate from Guillain-Barré is 10 percent, and I feared this thirty-eight-year-old woman would become a rare statistic. In my medical career—which spanned her lifetime—I had not seen a single case of Guillain-Barré.

However, this dreadful malady has been known for centuries. William Osler, regarded the father of modern medicine, described the features of this illness in 1892. He characterized it as an ascending paralyzing illness caused by the loss of the myelin sheath that covers the nerves and the axons, called a "demylenating inflammatory polyradiculoneuropathy." Three doctors working in the neurological center of the French Sixth Army in late August 1916 encountered two infantrymen "with motor difficulty, loss of deep tendon reflexes, numbness, and increased albumin in the spinal fluid."

Criteria for the diagnosis of Guillain-Barré remained controversial, as patients present with different symptoms of nerve damage, from eye disorders to paralysis of the entire body and death within thirty hours of onset.

Then came attempts to forestall the influenza Asian epidemic on a national scale in 1957, and the Hong Kong Flu in 1968. In the 70s President Ford issued a strong recommendation to the American public for a massive vaccination using a swine flu vaccine, issued by the CDC. The insurers refused to cover the liability for side effects because an entire population was going to be vaccinated.

Within ten weeks after the program was started, cases of Guillain-Barré were reported. Eventually thousands of cases appeared from coast to coast, and tens of millions of dollars were paid out by the government to the victims or their families.

The criteria for the proper diagnosis were somewhat defined after the vaccination debacle, but not the etiology of this terrible illness, or the acceptable treatment.

I sat by Lana's bedside as she became further paralyzed and approached death. For many years I had been the attending physician in the intensive care unit for thousands of patients, but never for someone I loved.

The infectious disease doctor suggested treating her with intravenous antibiotics for Lyme disease. The neurological team believed a compromised immune system was the cause of this disaster. Their objective was to remove the tyrant anti-globulin from the cells with intravenous gamma globulin.

As the hours ticked away, her breathing becoming weaker. We were ready at any moment to intubate her. If the central nervous system was attacked by the unknown agent, there would be no hope for her survival. Her entire respiratory and heart function would come to a sudden halt that would not respond to any outside intervention.

I saw Lana's move her lips in silent prayer as I clutched her hand.

By early morning her breathing had improved and she did not need to be intubated. She could speak and move her eyes and was able to swallow. But that was all. She had become a quadriplegic.

But each day there was some slight improvement, such as minor movements of her arms. Two weeks later her illness became stabilized and we could transfer her to the step-down intensive care unit.

The following week she was moved to the rehabilitation floor, which would become her home for the next four months. Her mother came up from Texas and was given a bed in her daughter's room.

Lana's brain was alert, but she had to be spoon-fed. Each day she asked the same question: "Will I ever be the same as before?"

"We are all praying for you," the head nurse would tell her.

An orderly transferred her from her bed to an armchair by means of a cage-like carrier called a Hoyer. This gentle orderly saw her despair and while he was swinging her in the air, would say *"My petit oiseau,* my little bird, where shall we land you today?"

"Tonight to Paris, to the Bistro Michelle."

So it went for weeks and weeks, Lana's never complaining but hoping and praying for recovery.

This illness is often preceded by a minor viral infection. Usually, a week or so after eating poorly cooked poultry, the episodes of diarrhea and fever and muscle pain follow. After the gastrointestinal illness subsides, paralysis sets in: numbness followed by an ascending paralysis, beginning in the lower legs. It may stop or swiftly proceed to the head, often causing respiratory paralysis not unlike polio. The author Joseph Heller suffered from this illness and wrote a masterful book about his long confinement. Allan Bloom, the writer and philosopher, also suffered from it.

After four months Lana's was discharged from the rehabilitation center to our home. Special ramps were built for wheelchair access, doors removed, special toilets installed, tub chairs for bathing, and a hospital bed. And an emergency button was installed but with a special flat cushion, as Lana's was unable to use her hands to call for help. Aides came twice a day to wash her. A physical therapist and an occupational therapist came daily. Our housekeeper did the shopping and I cooked dinner.

Today Lana's wears braces on her legs and is able to waddle along with a cane. Each week I see improvement, the result of her youthful strength and courage, as well as her extensive support systems. But she also suffers constant humiliation, for example, in restaurants that have no wheelchair access. Once or twice, strong young waiters had to lift her and the wheelchair to the dining room.

Her gastroenterologist, trying to determine how a healthy young woman with no immunologic tendencies or disorders could become brutally afflicted, deduced the probable cause: undercooked chicken served on our flight home from France. This causes one of the most serious forms of motor damage. Recovery is slow and many times incomplete because the basic element of the motor nerve (called the axon) becomes destroyed.

Lana's still can't perform everyday activities. Her hands are mere vestiges of their once beautiful appearance. She can write only slowly, as a child who just learned to use a pencil, forming large, uneven letters. Before this catastrophe she worked as my assistant, typing medical charts, articles, and books, and she was also employed as a legal secretary. But now she cannot type, open a jar, or switch on a lamp. When buying clothes she must rub the cloth against her face to feel its texture, as she has lost all feeling in her hands. Even with her leg braces, she cannot walk more than a few hundred yards because of muscle weakness, and she cannot climb stairs.

She will not be a mother. She will not work again. We travel together only with difficulty, as it's impossible for her to walk more than a little way. Nor can we keep up the active social schedule we used to enjoy. Lana's will remain disabled for as long as she lives.

Could I sue the airline whose convenient meal ruined the life of a healthy young woman? There would be no way to prove our case. And it wouldn't give Lana's her life back. We have moved past frustration and bitterness to a place of familiar companionship, looking back on that idyllic vacation in France with intense nostalgia and regret.

HOWDY, PARDNER

2005/2010

H E WAS DRESSED IN A GRAY SUIT, WHITE SHIRT, AND striped tie, and he stood erect as he entered my consulting office. I sat behind my antique desk and rose to greet him, looking into his pale face and brown eyes. He had been having chest pain. I sat down and began asking the usual questions: "Are you having any chest pain now? Can you tell me when was the last time you had chest pain?"

He did not answer. Was he deaf? Did he not understand the questions? He sat motionless as if in a trance, his eyes staring directly at me. His face became red as a cooked lobster. He moved his hands from the side and toward his pants as if trying to adjust their height and moved about in his chair, keeping his eyes fixed on me.

"Well," I asked in a friendly but anxious tone, "since you won't talk to me about your chest pain, tell me: What kind of work do you do—computers, sales, are you a builder?" He still stared at me, moving his hands to his fly and squirming in his seat, crossing his legs, stretching, and uncrossing them as if he were getting ready to sprint. I grew more and more uneasy. He stood up and now moved his hands away from the front of his pants and toward his wide brown leather belt with a silver buckle engraved with the image of a cowboy. He slowly undid his buckle and pulled the alligator leather belt free, like a snake unwinding.

I have known danger and the sense of being near death, and I sensed it here. I rushed past him out of my consulting room, saying, "I will be back in a jiff," and whispered to my secretary to call the police.

He remained standing, stretching his belt, looking toward the opened door and moving slowly toward me. His eyes widened like a wild beast about to attack his prey. In minutes the police were restraining him as he struggled, clutching his belt and swinging it like a lasso, trying to strike them. They managed to handcuff him after striking him firmly on his head with their night sticks. I stood aghast as he continued to stare at me with wild glaring eyes as they dragged him out of my office. The whole time he had not uttered a word or a shout of pain or protest.

They brought him to the emergency room, where he was hospitalized on the psychiatric unit.

Five years later, by which time thousands of new patients had consulted me for chest pain, the patient who threatened me with his belt appeared in my office again. He was elegantly dressed, spoke in a pleasant tone, and responded swiftly to my questions about his chest pain. His medical records were spread out in front of me on my desk. I did not remind him that he had consulted me five years ago for fear it might trigger another psychotic episode. As he spoke he fingered his belt, the same one with the large buckle and the cowboy insignia.

"I see you are looking at my belt," he said in a pleasant tone.

"Yes," I answered. "It is interesting."

"It belonged to my father. He was wearing it when he died of a heart attack. Now I wear it every day. And that is why I came to see you, to be sure I don't have a bad heart like him. You probably don't remember him. You saw him once in the hospital ten years ago."

He was right: I did not remember his father. Nor did he remember his threatening stance with me the last time I saw him.

We did a complete cardiac examination, which included a stress test, and found his heart to be normal. He had a normal lipid profile as well. When I gave him his results the following week, he was glad for the news and offered me the belt as a gesture of gratitude.

I still have the belt, and I still have the now-treated schizophrenic cowboy as a patient.

SIEGFRIED KRA
was born into a wealthy family in Danzig in 1930. After escaping from the Gestapo, they emigrated to New York, where Siegfried learned how to speak English without an accent. He attended CCNY, then went to medical school in France and Switzerland before completing his training in cardiology at Yale. In a half century of practice, he treated tens of thousands of patients, some of whom inspired his fictional story collections. Dr. Kra has published over a dozen books, including *What Every Woman Must Know About Heart Disease* from Warner Books, and *The Three-Legged Stallion* from W.W. Norton. His passions include opera, growing orchids, and tennis, which he still plays weekly at age eighty-nine. He also still teaches as an Associate Professor of Medicine at Yale University School of Medicine and at Quininipac University Netter School of Medicine.

CPSIA information can be obtained
at www.ICGtesting.com
Printed in the USA
FFHW011158260120
58015920-63157FF